Skills Link™

Everyday
Mathematics®

Skills Link™

Everyday
Mathematics®

Cumulative Practice Sets

Columbus, OH • Chicago, IL • Redmond, WA

The **McGraw·Hill** Companies

www.sra4kids.com

SRA

The **McGraw-Hill** Companies

Contents

Write all of your answers on a separate sheet of paper.

Write the letter of the line plot that makes sense with the survey question asked.

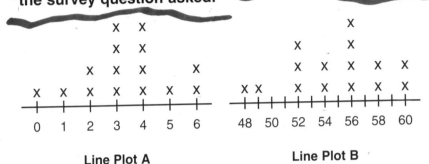

Line Plot A   Line Plot B

1. How many pieces of fruit do you eat each day?

2. How many inches tall are you?

Solve.

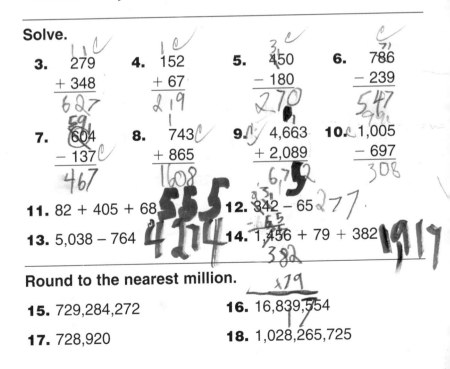

3. 279
    + 348

4. 152
    + 67

5. 450
    − 180

6. 786
    − 239

7. 604
    − 137

8. 743
    + 865

9. 4,663
    + 2,089

10. 1,005
    − 697

11. 82 + 405 + 68

12. 342 − 65

13. 5,038 − 764

14. 1,456 + 79 + 382

Round to the nearest million.

15. 729,284,272

16. 16,839,554

17. 728,920

18. 1,028,265,725

Write all of your answers on a separate sheet of paper.

Use digits to write the following numbers.

19. thirty-two thousand, four hundred fifty-nine

20. seven hundred thousand, thirty

21. eight hundred thousand, six hundred nine

Complete each pattern. Note: There may be more than one operation per pattern set.

22. 29, 34, 39, ■, 49, ■, ■

23. 73, ■, 57, 49, 41, ■, ■

24. 45, 48, 54, 57, ■, ■, 72

25. ■, ■, 40, 33, 29, 22

26. 19, 25, 20, ■, 21, ■, ■

27. -1, ■, $-3\frac{1}{2}$, ■, -6, $-7\frac{1}{4}$, ■, ■

Complete the "What's My Rule?" tables.

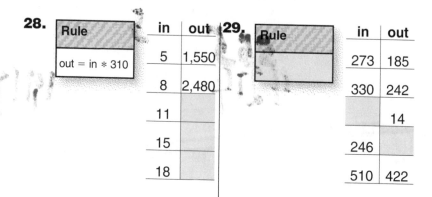

28.

Rule	in	out
out = in * 310	5	1,550
	8	2,480
	11	
	15	
	18	

29.

Rule	in	out
	273	185
	330	242
		14
	246	
	510	422

Practice Set 2

Write all of your answers on a separate sheet of paper.

Find the landmarks for the following set of numbers:

9, 10, 7, 19, 12, 8, 12, 12, 8, 9, 15

1. maximum **2.** minimum **3.** range

4. median **5.** mean **6.** mode

Solve.

7. 2,100
   − 736

8. 6,480
   + 827

9. 7,200
   − 3,300

10. 7,410
    − 680

11.   927
   + 1,294

12.   8,327
   + 13,056

13. 12,256
   − 8,236

14. 12,000
   − 3,000

Complete.

15. 2 yd = ■ in.

16. 30 in. = ■ ft

17. 24 ft = ■ yd

18. $4\frac{3}{4}$ ft = ■ in.

19. 6 yd 2 ft = ■ in.

20. 4 yd = ■ ft

21. 2 yd 2 ft = ■ ft

22. $6\frac{1}{2}$ yd = ■ in.

23. 8 yd $2\frac{1}{2}$ ft = ■ in.

24. 10 in. = ■ ft

25. 9 yd 1 in. = ■ in.

26. 60 in. = ■ ft

Write all of your answers on a separate sheet of paper.

As part of a survey, 25 girls and 25 boys were asked what their favorite chore was.

Number of Girls	Number of Boys	Favorite Chore
3	1	Wash dishes
4	4	Make the bed
5	6	Vacuum
5	8	Dust
2	2	Do laundry
6	4	Set the table

1. Make a bar graph to show the results of that survey.

2. Which chore was chosen as the favorite by the most girls? By the most boys?

The students decided to raise money for a field trip by doing chores for people. They earned $1 for each completed chore.

Day of the Week	Money Earned
Sunday	$57
Monday	$44
Tuesday	$39
Wednesday	$46
Thursday	$50
Friday	$61
Saturday	$72

3. Make a broken-line graph showing their earnings for a one-week period.

4. What is the mean, or average, number of dollars that the students earned each day?

Use with or after Lesson 1.6.

Write all of your answers on a separate sheet of paper.

Solve.

5. 3 * 60 = ■

6. 800 / ■ = 200

7. 150 / 3 = ■

8. ■ * 9 = 630

9. 40 * 80 = ■

10. 2,700 / 30 = ■

11. ■ / 20 = 60

12. 600 * ■ = 6,000

13. 50 * 400 = ■

14. 4,000 / ■ = 80

15. ■ * 60 = 48,000

16. ■ / 70 = 800

17. List in order from greatest to least.

$3\frac{2}{3}$, π, 3.5, $\frac{300}{100}$, $\frac{10}{3}$

Rewrite the numbers, and units, in the following statements so that they sound more reasonable.

> **Example** Alice said that it takes her about **900 seconds** to get to school in the morning.
>
> Answer: 900 seconds = 15 minutes

18. Richard's report stated that a giraffe can reach leaves on trees as tall as 240 inches.

19. Greta explained that a hippopotamus can eat 2,080 ounces of food in one night.

20. Angie made a chart of top running speeds for animals. The entry for the rhinoceros lists its running speed as 158,400 feet/hour.

21. Allan wrote on a height chart that he is 1,600 millimeters tall.

Practice Set 4

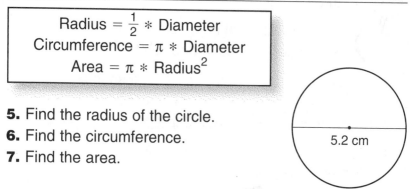

Write all of your answers on a separate sheet of paper.

The graph below shows the cost of a consultation with a computer specialist. Use the graph to answer the questions.

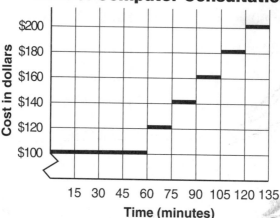

Cost of Computer Consultation

1. What is the cost of the first hour of the consultation?
2. After the first hour, what does each additional 15 minutes cost?
3. What would be the cost for a consultation lasting 1 hour and 5 minutes?
4. What would be the cost for a consultation lasting 2 hours and 15 minutes?

Radius $= \frac{1}{2}$ * Diameter
Circumference $= \pi$ * Diameter
Area $= \pi$ * Radius^2

5. Find the radius of the circle.
6. Find the circumference.
7. Find the area.

5.2 cm

Use with or after Lesson 1.7.

Write all of your answers on a separate sheet of paper.

The student council surveyed students about their favorite school lunch entrees. The results of the survey are displayed in the circle graph.

1. What percent of the students chose pizza? *50%*

2. Which lunch entree was chosen by 10% of the students? *chicken strips*

3. What percent of the students chose something other than pizza, burrito, or chicken strips? *15%*

50% Pizza

25% Burrito

Chicken Strips *10%*

Other *15%*

Solve.

4. 46
    * 7

5. 525
    * 6

6. 756
    * 8

7. 827
    * 9

8. 64
    * 73

9. 214
    * 48

10. 519
    * 73

11. 394
    * 15

12. 79 * 29

13. 143 * 82

14. 607 * 189

15. 326 * 160

List the factors of each number.

16. 18   **17.** 24   **18.** 36   **19.** 50

Write all of your answers on a separate sheet of paper.

Write the following numbers in digits.

20. forty-three trillion, six hundred eighty-one million, nine hundred

21. two billion, ninety-five million, five hundred thousand

22. six and fourteen-thousandths

Write the following numbers in words.

23. 2.08

24. 836,920,530

25. 65,321,070,000

26. 17,422.7

Determine the balance in each container below and then answer the questions that follow.

> ### *Example*
> Balance = −10
> If 16 ⊞ counters are added to the container, what is the new balance?
> Balance = +6
>
> 10⊞   20⊟

27. What is the balance?

28. If 8 ⊟ counters are added to the container, what is the new balance?

25⊞   18⊟
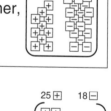

29. What is the balance?

30. If 11 ⊞ counters are added to the container, what is the new balance?

17⊞   26⊟
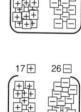

Write all of your answers on a separate sheet of paper.

Make name-collection boxes for the three numbers listed below. Use as many different kinds of numbers and operations as you can.

Example

$$18\frac{5}{9}$$

$$\frac{167}{9}$$

$$19 - \frac{8}{18}$$

$$9\frac{5}{18} * 2$$

1. 13

2. 79.5

3. $40\frac{3}{4}$

Find the perimeter and area of each figure.

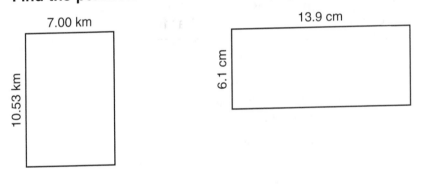

7.00 km

10.53 km

13.9 cm

6.1 cm

4. Perimeter

5. Area

6. Perimeter

7. Area

---

8. What numbers are divisible by 3?

543, 544, 545, 546, 547, 548, 549,
550, 551, 552, 553, 554, 555, 556,
557, 558

Write all of your answers on a separate sheet of paper.

Complete.

1. 1 pint = _____ cups

2. 64 fluid ounces = _____ quarts

3. 6 cups = _____ pints

4. 1 gallon = _____ cups

5. 40 quarts = _____ gallons

6. 48 fluid ounces = _____ cups

7. 3 pints = _____ fluid ounces

8. 12 quarts = _____ pints

Write a number sentence, and then solve.

9. A punch bowl holds 80 fluid ounces. How many pints of juice are needed to fill it?

10. Erika has a half-gallon of milk. How many 6-ounce glasses of milk can she serve? How much milk will be left over?

11. Ron mixed together 3 quarts of juice. How many fluid ounces of juice did he have in all?

Write the missing numbers for the number lines.

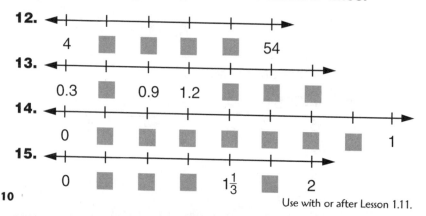

12. 4 ▨ ▨ ▨ ▨ 54

13. 0.3 ▨ 0.9 1.2 ▨ ▨ ▨

14. 0 ▨ ▨ ▨ ▨ ▨ ▨ ▨ 1

15. 0 ▨ ▨ ▨ $1\frac{1}{3}$ ▨ 2

Use with or after Lesson 1.11.

Write all of your answers on a separate sheet of paper.

Write the numbers in standard notation.

16. 3^2 **17.** 2^3 **18.** $\sqrt{100}$ **19.** 10^5

20. 10^0 **21.** 1^4 **22.** 4^2 **23.** $\sqrt{144}$

---

24. Use the clues to complete the puzzle.

- Divide 27 by 9. Add 1. Write the result in the thousands place.

- Multiply 8 ∗ 7. Subtract half of 100. Write the number in the hundreds place.

- Write the difference between 2^4 and 15 in the tenths place.

- Double the sum of the numbers in the thousands and hundreds place. Divide by 4. Write the result in the ones place.

- Triple the number in the tenths place. Subtract the result from the number in the ones place. Write the result in the tens place.

Divide. Write the result with the remainder.

	$21 \rightarrow R27$
Example	$37\overline{)804}$

25. $15\overline{)785}$ **26.** $27\overline{)612}$ **27.** $53\overline{)264}$ **28.** $31\overline{)976}$

29. $18\overline{)629}$ **30.** $22\overline{)320}$ **31.** $63\overline{)892}$ **32.** $16\overline{)701}$

Write all of your answers on a separate sheet of paper.

Solve.

1. 9.5
    + 5.6

2. 0.36
    + 0.15

3. 2.23
    − 1.69

4. 5.1
    − 0.82

5. 1.382
    + 6.2

6. 9.47
    − 5.81

7. 0.937
    − 0.324

8. 7.895
    + 4.162

9. 14.85
    − 1.46

10. 9.4 + 7.3 + 2.6

11. 1.3 + 2.6 + 5.9

12. 7.4 − 1.89

13. 5.26 − 3.17

Write *prime* or *composite* for each number.

14. 12

15. 17

16. 29

17. 46

18. 81

19. 99

Round each number to the nearest thousandth.

20. 9.0716

21. 38.65823

22. 129.9058

23. 74.5309

24. 2.46312

25. 40.5785

Write all of your answers on a separate sheet of paper.

Solve the pan-balance problems.

26. One coin weighs as much as ■ marbles.

27. One block weighs as much as ■ marbles.

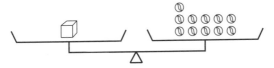

28. One ball weighs as much as ■ marbles.

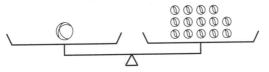

29. How many marbles would you need to place on the right pan to balance the two pans?

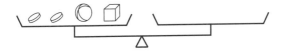

Make name-collection boxes for the numbers below. Use as many different kinds of numbers and operations as you can.

Example

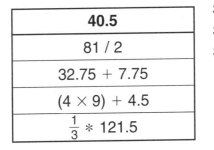

40.5
81 / 2
32.75 + 7.75
(4 × 9) + 4.5
$\frac{1}{3}$ ∗ 121.5

30. 29.2

31. 16.08

32. 22.76

Write all of your answers on a separate sheet of paper.

Write the best estimate for each product.

1. 14.9 * 6.7   10   100   1,000

2. 840.5 * 0.4   4   40   400

3. 3.76 * 1.91   8   80   800

4. 78.94 * 0.03   3   30   300

5. 176.4 * 12.4   200   2,000   20,000

6. 783.06 * 1.05   80   800   8,000

Multiply.

7.   9.5
      * 5.6

8.   7.3
      * 0.5

9.   14.9
      * 1.8

10.   26.9
      * 2.3

11.   9.3
      * 0.6

12.   57
      * 3.2

Solve each problem. Then write a number sentence.

13. Alex ordered 3 dozen pens for $1.39 each. What was the total cost of the order, not including tax?

14. Find the area of a square with sides 5.7 cm in length.

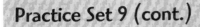
Write all of your answers on a separate sheet of paper.

Complete the "What's My Rule?" tables.

15.

Rule	in	out
out = in + 27	19	
	36	
	84	
	127	
	169	

16.

Rule	in	out
	31	7
	48	24
		29
	72	
		56

17.

Rule	in	out
	3	90
	8	240
	10	
		360
	20	

18.

Rule	in	out
out = in / 8	24	
		8
	720	
		40
	4,800	

Solve.

19. When Beth woke up, the temperature was −6°F outside. By the time she got home from school, the temperature was 19°F outside. How many degrees had the temperature risen during the day?

20. The temperature in Milwaukee at 6 P.M. was 28°F. By midnight the temperature had dropped 37 degrees. What was the temperature at midnight?

Practice Set 10

Write all of your answers on a separate sheet of paper.

Multiply.

1. $80 * 0.1$ 2. $12 * 0.01$

3. $77 * 0.001$ 4. $9.4 * 0.1$

5. $0.06 * 10$ 6. $28.6 * 100$

7. $0.7 * 0.1$ 8. $40 * 0.01$

9. $3.7 * 1,000$ 10. $7.1 * 0.1$

Solve.

11. $1,856 - (320 + 1,105)$ 12. $78 * (12 - 7)$

13. $4,189 + 2,326 + 1,190$ 14. $25 + (249 / 3)$

15. Mary is having a birthday party. How many $9 pizzas can she buy with $60?

16. Compact disks are on sale for $13 each, including tax. How many CDs can you buy with $55?

Round each number to the nearest tenth.

17. 36.981 18. 8.674 19. 20.85

20. 49.95 21. 17.312 22. 102.56

Measure the line segments to the nearest $\frac{1}{4}$ inch.

23. •————————————————————•

24. •——————————————————•

Write all of your answers on a separate sheet of paper.

Write the following numbers in standard notation.

1. 6 million
3. 1.4 trillion
5. 19 billion
7. 175 million

2. 0.2 billion
4. 30 million
6. 27.5 million
8. 4.6 million

Write the following numbers in number-and-word notation.

9. 1,300,000
11. 6,000,000,000

10. 39,000,000
12. 12,900,000,000

Complete the "What's My Rule?" tables.

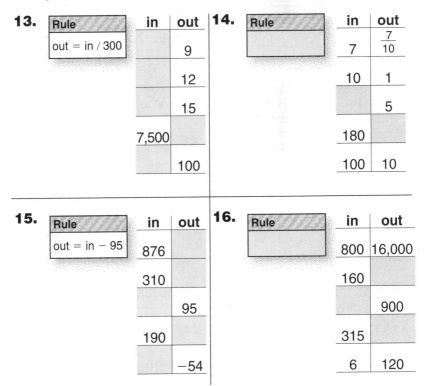

13.

Rule	in	out
out = in / 300		9
		12
		15
	7,500	
		100

14.

Rule	in	out
	7	$\frac{7}{10}$
	10	1
		5
	180	
	100	10

15.

Rule	in	out
out = in − 95	876	
	310	
		95
	190	
		−54

16.

Rule	in	out
	800	16,000
	160	
		900
	315	
	6	120

Write all of your answers on a separate sheet of paper.

17. Write each fraction as a decimal and a percent.

Fraction	$\frac{1}{2}$	$\frac{1}{4}$	$\frac{1}{5}$	$\frac{1}{10}$	$\frac{3}{4}$	$\frac{7}{10}$	$\frac{1}{3}$	$\frac{7}{8}$
Decimal	▣	▣	▣	▣	▣	▣	▣	▣
Percent	▣	▣	▣	▣	▣	▣	▣	▣

Make stem-and-leaf plots for the following groups.

Example 4, 21, 16, 7, 11,	**Stems**	**Leaves**
8, 22, 9, 16, 10,	**(10s)**	**(1s)**
9, 12, 16, 16	0	4, 7, 8, 9, 9
	1	0, 1, 2, 6, 6, 6, 6
	2	1, 2

102, 120, 94, 96, 80, 87, 94, 79, 82, 121, 91, 115, 120, 94, 76

18.

Stems (10s)	Leaves (1s)
7	
8	
9	
10	
11	
12	

19. What is the mode?

20. What is the median?

21. What is the range?

28, 24, 38, 41, 52, 29, 33, 43, 24, 56, 27, 58, 21, 39, 44, 55

22.

Stems (10s)	Leaves (1s)
2	
3	
4	
5	

23. What is the mode?

24. What is the median?

25. What is the range?

Use with or after Lesson 2.5.

SRB
27
139–141

Write all of your answers on a separate sheet of paper.

Write each number in words.

1. 0.9   **2.** 1.02   **3.** 23.015

4. 0.785   **5.** 0.89   **6.** 5.0677

Write the digits for each number.

7. seventy-two hundredths

8. ninety and six tenths

9. one thousand twenty-five and fifteen hundredths

10. two and six hundred seventy-five thousandths

11. one and two hundred thirty-eight thousandths

Use the graph to solve the problems.

12. During training, many athletes eat up to 6,000 calories per day. The recommended diet for most people is 2,000 calories per day. About how many times more calories do athletes eat during training than does the average person?

13. What percent of an athlete's calories comes from fat?

14. How many calories of an athlete's diet come from protein?

15. How many calories come from carbohydrates?

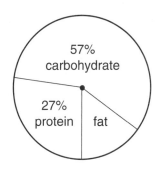

57% carbohydrate

27% protein   fat

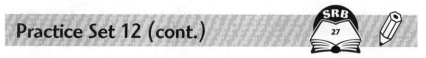
Write all of your answers on a separate sheet of paper.

16. Complete the *Powers of 10* table.

Thousands	Hundreds	Tens	Ones	.	Tenths	Hundredths	Thousandths
1,000	100	■	■	.	■	0.01	■
■	10 [10s]	■	10[1/10s]	.	10[1/100s]	■	10 [1/10,000s]
■	■	$10 * 1$	$10 * 1/10$	.	$10 * 1/100$	$10 * 1/1,000$	■
10^3	■	■	10^0	.	10^{-1}	■	10^{-3}

Write all of your answers on a separate sheet of paper.

Write each number in scientific notation.

1. 5,240,000

2. 10,600,000,000

3. 4,500,000

4. 23,000,000,000

5. 9,000,000,000,000

6. 140,000,000,000

Write each number in standard notation.

7. $3.2 * 10^5$

8. $4.0 * 10^7$

9. $1.23 * 10^8$

10. $6.12 * 10^6$

11. $5.0 * 10^9$

12. $2.5 * 10^{10}$

Write the next three numbers in each pattern.

13. 11, 26, 41

14. 865, 870, 875

15. 44, 56, 68

16. $2\frac{1}{2}$, $2\frac{3}{4}$, 3

17. A number has

1 in the billions place
6 in the hundred-thousands place
4 in the ten-billions place
2 in the thousands place
5 in the hundred-millions place
0 in the rest of the places

Write the number.

Rename as a mixed number.

18. $\frac{21}{2}$

19. $\frac{17}{3}$

20. $\frac{35}{4}$

21. $\frac{20}{9}$

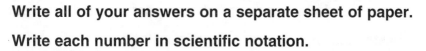
Write all of your answers on a separate sheet of paper.

Write each number in scientific notation.

1. 0.0021

2. 0.0009

3. 0.0152

4. 0.702

5. 50 thousand

6. 385,000

Write each number in standard notation.

7. $6 * 10^4$

8. $3.6 * 10^{-2}$

9. $8 * 10^{-4}$

10. $2.6 * 10^{-5}$

11. $1.38 * 10^7$

12. $5.8 * 10^6$

Use a calculator to solve. Write the answer in scientific notation.

13. $40^3 * 2^2$

14. $800^2 * 6^3$

15. $60^4 * 7$

16. $90^3 * 10^5$

Answer the questions about the figures below.

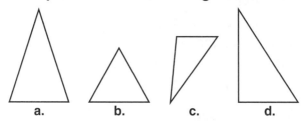

a.   b.   c.   d.

17. Which triangle looks like an isosceles triangle?

18. Which do you think has a right angle?

19. Which looks like an equilateral triangle?

20. Which triangle has more than one line of symmetry?

Use with or after Lesson 2.9.

SRB
22–24
200

Write all of your answers on a separate sheet of paper.

Estimate the quotient. Write a number sentence to show how you estimated.

1. 482 / 8

2. 821 / 17

3. 293 / 14

4. 626 / 7

5. 2,762 / 72

6. 1,456 / 29

Solve. Write answers with remainders.

7. 22)8,136

8. 10)4,478

9. 26)1,962

10. 32)714

11. 11)852

12. 5)90

13. Cole has $6.25 to buy school supplies. He wants one pack of pens for $1.15, a folder for $2.67, and a pack of paper for 99¢. How much money will he have left over? Write a number model for this problem.

14. Rosita bought four new books for a total of $32.65. What was the average cost per book?

Answer the following:

15. Find the radius of the circle.

16. Find the circumference.

17. Find the area.

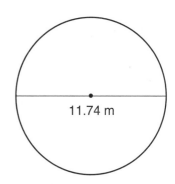

11.74 m

Write all of your answers on a separate sheet of paper.

Use the following list of numbers to answer the questions:

14, 18, 19, 13, 20, 13.5, 7.25, 19, 11.25

18. What is the range?   **19.** What is the mode?

20. What is the median?   **21.** What is the mean?

22. Complete the table.

Product	Exponential Notation	Standard Notation
11 * 11 * 11 * 11	▩	▩
▩	$12^{▩}$	1,728
▩	$▩^{14}$	16,384
▩	10^{15}	▩
18 * 18 * 18 * 18 * 18	▩	▩

23. Write the largest number you can with
the following digits:
2, 8, 6, 7, 2, 0, 2, 8, 3, 8, 3, 5, 1, 6, 0

Rewrite the number sentences with parentheses to make them correct.

24. $250 = 10 * 57 - 32$
25. $6 * 12 + 8 - 3 = 102$
26. $521 = 11 * 19 + 312$
27. $12 * 30 - 5 = 300$
28. $4.8 + 2.2 - 5 = 2$
29. $7.25 + 1.25 * 2 + 4.25 = 14$
30. $56 / 2.3 + 5.7 * 12 = 84$

Write all of your answers on a separate sheet of paper.

Estimate each quotient. Write a number sentence to show how you estimated.

1. 14.4 / 3

2. 83.6 / 4

3. 47.72 / 11

4. 33.1 / 7

5. 89.7 / 9

6. 52.6 / 6

Divide. Round to the nearest hundredth.

7. 29 / 7

8. 35 / 3

9. 51 / 9

10. 70 / 8

11. 64 / 6

12. 47 / 9

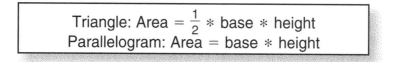

Triangle: Area $= \frac{1}{2} *$ base $*$ height
Parallelogram: Area $=$ base $*$ height

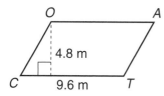

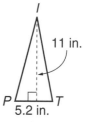

13. What is the name of the figure?

15. What is the name of the figure?

14. What is its area?

16. What is its area?

Write all of your answers on a separate sheet of paper.

Write the words for the following numbers.

17. 62,093,070

18. 11,263,750,000,000

19. 49,034,520,000,000

20. 560.8034

Complete the number lines.

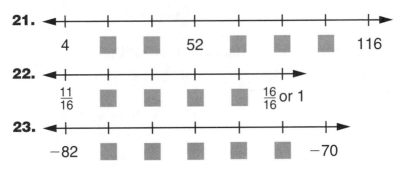

21. 4 ▨ ▨ 52 ▨ ▨ ▨ 116

22. $\frac{11}{16}$ ▨ ▨ ▨ ▨ $\frac{16}{16}$ or 1

23. −82 ▨ ▨ ▨ ▨ ▨ −70

Complete.

24. $2^8 = $ ▨

25. $4^{■} = 256$

26. $8 * 8 * 8 * 8 * 8 * 8 = 8^{■}$

27. The square root of 256 = ▨.

28. y to the third power $= y^{■}$

Draw the next picture.

29. •   • •. •.•.
              •   • • •

30. ‖•   ═   •‖
          •

Write all of your answers on a separate sheet of paper.

Write the letter of the special case which matches each general pattern.

1. $a(3 + 7) = (a * 3) + (a * 7)$

2. $n^3 = n * n * n$

3. $a + 0 = a$

4. $x + 2 = 2 + x$

5. $3(x - 5) = 3x - 15$

6. $\frac{1}{x} + \frac{1}{x} = \frac{2}{x}$

A. $7^3 = 7 * 7 * 7$

B. $3(21 - 5) = (3 * 21) - 15$

C. $17 + 2 = 2 + 17$

D. $5(3 + 7) = (5 * 3) + (5 * 7)$

E. $\frac{1}{5} + \frac{1}{5} = \frac{2}{5}$

F. $42 + 0 = 42$

Solve. (You may use a calculator for Problems 7–12.)

7. $6^5 * 1^5 = \blacksquare$

8. $7^2 - 2^3 = \blacksquare$

9. $9^2 - 3^3 = \blacksquare$

10. $14^2 + 10^3 = \blacksquare$

11. $20^2 * 2^4 = \blacksquare$

12. $2^{24} - 24^2 = \blacksquare$

13. $6^3 / 6^2 = \blacksquare$

14. $8^2 * 8^3 = 8^{\blacksquare}$

15. Charlotte earns $6.00 per week for mowing two neighbors' lawns. She pays her brother Sam 50¢ to pick up grass clippings for compost. After she pays her brother, how much money will she make in 7 weeks?

16. Suppose Charlotte doubled the number of lawns she mowed and also doubled the amount she earned in a week. Should she increase the amount she gives her brother, and if so, by how much? Explain.

Write all of your answers on a separate sheet of paper.

For each set of special cases, write a number sentence with two variables to describe the general pattern.

1. 3(15 + 9) = (3 * 15) + (3 * 9)
3(5 + 1) = (3 * 5) + (3 * 1)
3(0.25 + 0.75) = (3 * 0.25) + (3 * 0.75)

2. 10 * (2 * 4) = 2 * (10 * 4)
10 * (8 * 5) = 8 * (10 * 5)
10 * (0.3 * 0.8) = 0.3 * (10 * 0.8)

3. 0.4(1.05 − 3) = (0.4 * 1.05) − (0.4 * 3)
0.4(5.23 − 1.7) = (0.4 * 5.23) − (0.4 * 1.7)
0.4(17 − 6) = (0.4 * 17) − (0.4 * 6)

Use digits to write the following numbers:

4. nine and twenty-three hundredths

5. sixteen and four-ninths

6. eleven and four hundred eighteen thousandths

Complete each pattern. Note: There may be more than one operation per pattern set.

7. 12, 15, 11, 14, ■, ■, 9

8. ■, ■, 46, 36, 26, ■, ■

9. 54, 59, 67, ■, 80, ■, ■, ■

10. 29, 34, 39, ■, 49, ■, ■

11. 14, ■, 16, 8, 18, ■, ■, 12

Use with or after Lesson 3.2.

Write all of your answers on a separate sheet of paper.

Solve.

12.   59
        $* 59$

13. $33\overline{)835}$

14.   28
        $* 25$

15. $71\overline{)390}$

16. $97\overline{)4,598}$ **17.** $6\overline{)395}$

18.   200
        $* 56$

19. $46\overline{)3,318}$

20. Coach Rivera wants to put the 76 sixth graders in teams for a volleyball tournament. How many teams of 9 can he form?

21. Javier was married at the age of 28. In 3 more years, he will have been married 25 years. How old is Javier?

Complete.

22. $10^{10} = \blacksquare$

23. $10^{\blacksquare} = 10,000,000,000,000$

24. $100 * 100 * 100 * 100 * 100 = 10^{\blacksquare}$

25. $10 * 10^2 = 10^{\blacksquare} = \blacksquare$

Round each number to the nearest thousandth.

26. 3.9025   **27.** 78.2953

28. 3.2871   **29.** 6.0208

30. 3.4798   **31.** 26.2149

Tell whether each number is *prime* or *composite*.

32. 31   **33.** 57   **34.** 111   **35.** 19

Write all of your answers on a separate sheet of paper.

Write an algebraic expression for each situation. Use the suggested variable.

1. Virginia has 7 more rubber stamps than Melinda. If Melinda has r rubber stamps, how many rubber stamps does Virginia have?

2. Marco's dog weighs p pounds. Cody's dog weighs 5 pounds less. How much does Cody's dog weigh?

3. On Monday, Ellen sold 3 pumpkins. The next day she sold m more pumpkins. How many did she sell in all?

Write *true* or *false* for each number sentence.

4. $(3 + 4) * 3 = 21$

5. $42 = (54 / 9) * 7$

6. $7 * (6 + 3) = (40 / 5) * (17 - 9)$

7. $(48 / 8) / 2 < 10$

8. $(7 * 8) - 3 = 55$

Solve.

9. $905 - 238$

10. $847 - 460$

11. $957 - 249$

12. $3,688 + 9,375$

13. $85,387 + 47,967$

14. $9,651 - 850$

15. $381 + 429$

16. $2,109 + 762$

17. $15,038 - 27,864$

18. $9,080 + 799 + 225$

19. $90 + 569 + 77$

20. $4,896 - (658 + 1,900)$

Write all of your answers on a separate sheet of paper.

Complete the "What's My Rule?" tables.

1.

Rule	in	out
out = in * 4	60	240
	16	
		340
	11	
		142

2.

Rule	in	out
0.3 * in = out	30	9
		0.15
	105	
	393	
	705	

3.

Rule	in	out
in − 175 = out	600	
	112	
		35
	10	
		−82

4.

Rule	in	out
	8	16
	14	28
		45
	35	
	40.2	80.4

Rename as a fraction.

5. $6\frac{1}{5}$ **6.** $3\frac{3}{8}$ **7.** $4\frac{1}{2}$ **8.** $1\frac{16}{24}$

9. $10\frac{12}{13}$ **10.** $5\frac{2}{5}$ **11.** $7\frac{2}{9}$ **12.** $24\frac{2}{3}$

13. $10\frac{2}{5}$ **14.** $4\frac{6}{7}$ **15.** $21\frac{3}{5}$ **16.** $14\frac{1}{6}$

17. $18\frac{1}{9}$ **18.** $9\frac{1}{3}$ **19.** $11\frac{1}{8}$ **20.** $3\frac{14}{15}$

Practice Set 20 (cont.)

Write all of your answers on a separate sheet of paper.

Estimate each product. Write a number sentence to show how you estimated.

21. 12.3 * 5.6

22. 1.35 * 27.9

23. 261.95 * 32.8

24. 2.39 * 682

25. 86.74 * 4.18

26. 126.9 * 4.56

27. 7.893 * 12.008

28. 981 * 1.73

Answer the following questions:

29. What is the prime factorization of 24?

   2 * 3 * 5   2 * 2 * 2 * 3   2 * 12   2 * 2 * 3 * 3

30. What is the prime factorization of 72?

   2 * 5 * 5   2 * 36   2 * 2 * 2 * 3 * 3

31. What is the prime factorization of 77?

   2 * 5 * 7   3 * 3 * 3 * 3   7 * 11   2 * 6 * 6

32. What are the prime factors for 105?

33. What number is represented by the prime factors 3 * 5 * 5 * 13?

Use the following list of numbers to answer the questions.

   10, 8.5, 11, 9, 10.5, 10.5, 7, 13, 10.5

34. What is the range?

35. What is the mode?

36. What is the median?

37. What is the mean?

38. If you disregard the highest and lowest numbers, how would that affect the mean? Do you think this would be a *more* or *less* accurate representation of the numbers? Explain.

SRB
107–110

Write all of your answers on a separate sheet of paper.

Complete the rate tables below. Then answer the questions.

Example A company can produce 800 widgets per day.

widgets	800	1,600	2,400	3,200	4,000
days	1	2	3	4	5

1. How many widgets can the factory produce in $3\frac{1}{2}$ days?

2. How many 5-day weeks will it take to produce 16,000 widgets?

On the highway, Alec's car gets 28 miles per gallon of gasoline.

3.

miles	28	▪	▪	▪	▪	...	▪
gallons	1	2	3	4	5	...	12

4. His parent's house is 100 miles away by the nearest highway. How many gallons of gasoline will Alec need to get there?

5. The gas tank holds 12 gallons. How many times will Alec need to stop for gas on a road trip of 340 miles?

In the city, Alec's car gets 23 miles per gallon of gasoline.

6.

miles	23	▪	▪	▪	▪	...	▪
gallons	1	2	3	4	5	...	12

7. How far can the car go in the city on 4.25 gallons?

8. Alec drives about 425 miles in the city each month. How many gallons does he buy in a month?

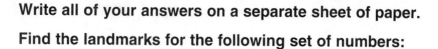

Write all of your answers on a separate sheet of paper.

Find the landmarks for the following set of numbers:

4, 3, 6, 2.5, 3, 2.25, 1.5, 7, 4, 6.75

9. maximum　　**10.** minimum　　**11.** range

12. median　　**13.** mean　　**14.** mode

Solve.

15. $9 * 10^{-2} = $ ■

16. $50 * 10^{■} = 0.5$

17. $54 = 10^{■} * 0.054$

18. $42,000 = 7 * 6 * 10^{■}$

19. $10^{■} * 1,500 = 0.15$

20. $10^{■} * 8,306 = 0.8306$

Round to the nearest million.

21. 386,905,817,009

22. 9,632,928,025

23. 65,837,296,702

24. 9,027,583

25. 782,660,327

26. 2,396,920,275

Write each number in standard notation.

27. 0.5 million

28. 700 thousand

29. 1.9 billion

30. 5.2 trillion

31. 67 billion

32. 100 trillion

33. 3 million

34. 0.2 trillion

Write all of your answers on a separate sheet of paper.

Use the spreadsheet to answers questions 1–4.

1. What is in cell A2?

2. What is in cell B4?

3. Which cell contains the word "total"?

4. Write a formula for calculating cell B8 that uses the cell names.

	A	B
		Records
	A	**B**
1	Day	Sales
2	Monday	$4.25
3	Tuesday	$9.50
4	Wednesday	$8.25
5	Thursday	$6.50
6	Friday	$12.75
7		
8	Total	$41.24

Find the least common multiple for each pair of numbers.

5. 8, 10   **6.** 2, 7   **7.** 9, 12

8. 5, 6   **9.** 10, 15   **10.** 9, 15

Solve. Write answers with remainders for division problems.

11. $4\overline{)496}$ **12.** $6\overline{)283}$ **13.** $8\overline{)2,419}$ **14.** $\begin{array}{r} 323 \\ * 8 \\ \hline \end{array}$

15. $\begin{array}{r} 687 \\ * 12 \\ \hline \end{array}$ **16.** $5\overline{)325}$ **17.** $44\overline{)505}$ **18.** $\begin{array}{r} 784 \\ - 531 \\ \hline \end{array}$

19. $\begin{array}{r} 1,026 \\ - 296 \\ \hline \end{array}$ **20.** $36\overline{)623}$ **21.** $5\overline{)225}$ **22.** $\begin{array}{r} 825 \\ + 369 \\ \hline \end{array}$

Write all of your answers on a separate sheet of paper.

Add.

1. $7 + (-6)$

2. $19 + (-7)$

3. $-11 + (-5)$

4. $9 + (-4)$

5. $8 + (-9)$

6. $-14 + (-2)$

7. $-20 + 7$

8. $-12 + (-12)$

Find the greatest common factor for each pair of numbers.

9. 12, 30

10. 6, 16

11. 16, 24

12. 18, 29

13. 21, 15

14. 32, 50

Ellen made a table of sales from her farm stand.

15. Make a broken-line graph showing the sales for Weeks 1–6.

16. Which week had the greatest sales?

17. What were the sales for Week 1?

Week	Sales
1	$150
2	$250
3	$300
4	$325
5	$350
6	$275

18. How much greater were the sales for Week 6 than for Week 1?

19. What was the mean number of dollars for the 6 weeks?

Write all of your answers on a separate sheet of paper.

Solve.

20. 1,254
     * 50

21. 4,235
     − 1,227

22. 1,675
     − 885

23. 8,263
     + 7,582

24. 82.4
     + 33.9

25. 11.7
     − 18.5

26. 500
     * 7.6

27. 5,345
     − 4,226

28. 4,321
     − 2,636

29. 71.4
     + 22.8

30. 30.9
     − 18.4

31. 22.8
     * 11

Complete the number lines.

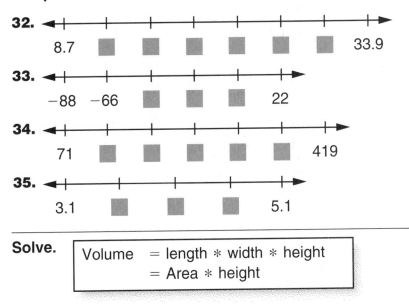

32. 8.7 ⬛ ⬛ ⬛ ⬛ ⬛ ⬛ 33.9

33. −88 −66 ⬛ ⬛ ⬛ 22

34. 71 ⬛ ⬛ ⬛ ⬛ ⬛ 419

35. 3.1 ⬛ ⬛ ⬛ 5.1

Solve.

> Volume = length * width * height
> = Area * height

Each rectangular prism has a volume of 60 cubic inches. What is the height of each prism?

36.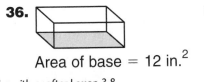

Area of base = 12 in.²

37.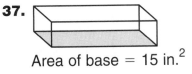

Area of base = 15 in.²

Practice Set 24

Write all of your answers on a separate sheet of paper.

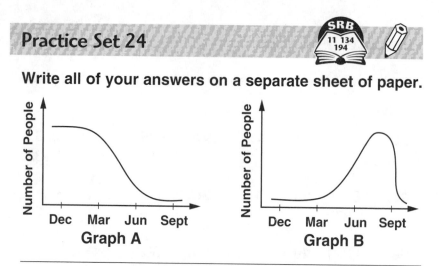

Graph A

Graph B

Write the letter of the graph that best fits the description.

1. This graph represents the number of people who are camping at a state beach park in California.

2. This graph represents the number of people who are staying at a ski resort in New Hampshire.

The perimeter of a square can be found by the formula $p = 4 * s$. Find the perimeter of a square with

3. $s = 7$ inches

4. $s = 3.5$ meters

5. $s = 0.2$ kilometers

6. $s = 2\frac{1}{2}$ miles

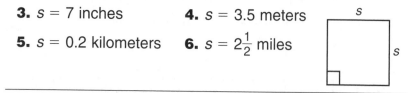

Use the numbers from 100 to 120 to answer the following questions.

7. Which numbers are divisible by 5?

8. Which numbers are divisible by 3?

9. Which numbers are divisible by 6?

10. Which numbers are prime?

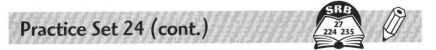
Write all of your answers on a separate sheet of paper.

Complete the "What's My Rule?" tables.

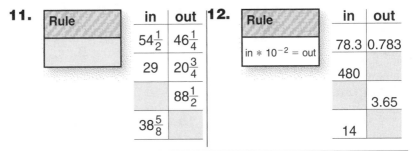

11.

Rule	in	out
	$54\frac{1}{2}$	$46\frac{1}{4}$
	29	$20\frac{3}{4}$
		$88\frac{1}{2}$
	$38\frac{5}{8}$	

12.

Rule	in	out
in * 10^{-2} = out	78.3	0.783
	480	
		3.65
	14	

Rewrite the number sentences with parentheses to make them correct.

13. $8.4 = 7 * 2 - 0.8$

14. $336 - 26 - 29 = 339$

15. $7 * 3.4 + 5 = 58.8$

16. $7 * 3.4 + 5 = 28.8$

17. Use the clues to complete the puzzle.

___ ___ ___ . ___ ___ ___

- Add 53 and 37. Divide by 10 and write the result in the ones place.

- Quadruple the number in the ones place and divide by 6. Write the result in the tenths place.

- Multiply 31 * 8. Subtract 241. Write the result in the thousandths place.

- Subtract the number in the tenths place from 54 and divide by 6. Write the result in the hundredths place.

- Find $\frac{5}{8}$ of 8. Write the result in the tens place.

- Subtract the product of 6 * 16 from 100. Write the result in the hundreds place.

Write all of your answers on a separate sheet of paper.

Write each fraction in simplest form.

1. $\frac{6}{12}$ **2.** $\frac{75}{100}$ **3.** $\frac{4}{6}$ **4.** $\frac{2}{8}$

5. $\frac{10}{24}$ **6.** $\frac{26}{50}$ **7.** $\frac{5}{15}$ **8.** $\frac{18}{24}$

Compare. Write <, >, or =.

9. $6 * 10^5$ ■ 600,000 **10.** $1.25 * 10^{-2}$ ■ 0.25

11. 9.5 million ■ 950,000 **12.** $3 * 10^7$ ■ 3,500,000

13. $5.23 * 10^7$ ■ 53 billion **14.** 0.057 ■ $5.7 * 10^{-3}$

Find the volume of each rectangular prism.

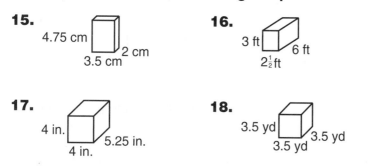

15.
4.75 cm
2 cm
3.5 cm

16.
3 ft
6 ft
$2\frac{1}{2}$ ft

17.
4 in.
5.25 in.
4 in.

18.
3.5 yd
3.5 yd
3.5 yd

Solve.

19. $(-43) + (-98) = y$ **20.** $(+264) + (-154) = J$

21. $r + (+153) = (-632)$ **22.** $M = (-25) + (-84)$

Write all of your answers on a separate sheet of paper.

Compare. Write <, >, or =.

1. $\frac{1}{6}$ < $\frac{2}{5}$

2. $\frac{2}{3}$ > $\frac{5}{8}$

3. $\frac{2}{9}$ < $\frac{7}{12}$

4. $\frac{3}{10}$ < $\frac{1}{4}$

5. $\frac{5}{12}$ = $\frac{10}{24}$

6. $\frac{1}{4}$ < $\frac{3}{7}$

7. $\frac{8}{9}$ > $\frac{9}{11}$

8. $\frac{5}{25}$ = $\frac{1}{5}$

Add, using mental math.

9. $-5 + 7$ 2

10. $-20 + 6$ -14

11. $15 + (-8)$ 7

12. $-3 + (-7)$ -4

13. $10 + (-17)$ 7

14. $-6 + 9$ 3

15. $-5 + -4$ 1

16. $-9 + -6$ 3

Complete the "What's My Rule?" tables.

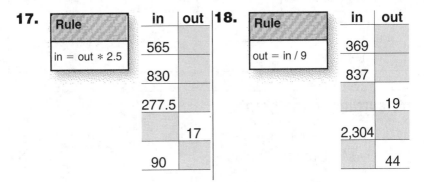

17.

Rule	in	out
in = out * 2.5	565	
	830	
	277.5	
		17
	90	

18.

Rule	in	out
out = in / 9	369	
	837	
		19
	2,304	
		44

Practice Set 27

SRB 27 69 78

Write all of your answers on a separate sheet of paper.

Add or subtract. Write your answers as fractions in simplest form.

1. $\frac{1}{3} + \frac{5}{12}$

2. $\frac{5}{6} - \frac{1}{12}$

3. $\frac{7}{8} - \frac{3}{16}$

4. $\frac{1}{2} + \frac{1}{10}$

5. $\frac{3}{10} + \frac{4}{5}$

6. $\frac{11}{12} - \frac{1}{6}$

7. $\frac{1}{2} + \frac{1}{2} + \frac{1}{4}$

8. $\frac{3}{5} + \frac{1}{2} + \frac{1}{10}$

9. Complete the table.

Words	Standard Notation	Exponential Notation
one-tenth	0.1	10^{-1}
▪	0.01	▪
one-thousandth	▪	▪
one-millionth	▪	▪
▪	▪	10^{-9}
one-trillionth	▪	▪

According to the graph:

10. What season is preferred by Mr. Crowder's class?

11. What percent of the class does NOT prefer spring?

Use with or after Lesson 4.3.

Write all of your answers on a separate sheet of paper.

Solve.

12. 82,416 **13.** 6,375 **14.** 233 **15.** 5.83
+ 15,249 * 53 * 61 * 4.2

16. 9.457 **17.** 3.907 **18.** 43 **19.** 33.90
− 3.363 − 1.478 * 2.6 + 12.05

20. 1.907 **21.** 634.98 **22.** 3)1.80 **23.** 8)71.2
+ 90.640 − 112.90

24. 9)40.5 **25.** 18,323 **26.** 9.76 **27.** 167.06
+ 21,475 * 7.3 * 0.04

Fill in the missing numbers on the number lines.

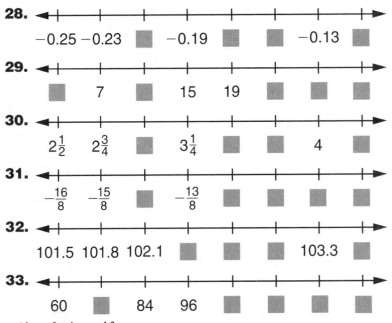

28. −0.25 −0.23 ▉ −0.19 ▉ ▉ −0.13 ▉

29. ▉ 7 ▉ 15 19 ▉ ▉ ▉

30. $2\frac{1}{2}$ $2\frac{3}{4}$ ▉ $3\frac{1}{4}$ ▉ ▉ 4 ▉

31. $-\frac{16}{8}$ $-\frac{15}{8}$ ▉ $-\frac{13}{8}$ ▉ ▉ ▉ ▉

32. 101.5 101.8 102.1 ▉ ▉ ▉ 103.3 ▉

33. 60 ▉ 84 96 ▉ ▉ ▉ ▉

Write all of your answers on a separate sheet of paper.

Add or subtract.

1. $4\frac{1}{5}$
$+ 3\frac{2}{5}$

2. 6
$- 1\frac{1}{4}$

3. $10\frac{1}{6}$
$- 4\frac{5}{6}$

4. $2\frac{1}{8}$
$+ 1\frac{7}{8}$

5. $7\frac{2}{3}$
$+ 4\frac{2}{3}$

6. $9\frac{1}{4}$
$- 6\frac{3}{4}$

7. $5\frac{1}{3}$
$- 1\frac{1}{3}$

8. 10
$+ 2\frac{2}{7}$

9. $8\frac{1}{5}$
$- 2\frac{3}{5}$

Find the missing number.

10. $\frac{2}{3} = \frac{a}{30}$

11. $\frac{5}{12} = \frac{x}{48}$

12. $\frac{7}{10} = \frac{c}{50}$

13. $\frac{7}{25} = \frac{d}{100}$

14. $\frac{5}{6} = \frac{r}{42}$

15. $\frac{2}{9} = \frac{t}{45}$

Determine the balance in each container below.

16. What is the balance?

17. If 18 ⊟ counters are added to the container, what is the new balance?

18. What is the balance?

19. If 7 ⊞ counters are removed from the container, what is the new balance?

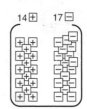

Practice Set 29

Write all of your answers on a separate sheet of paper.

Add or subtract.

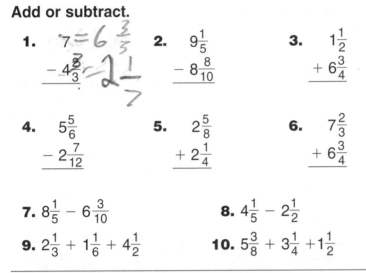

1. $7 = 6\frac{3}{5}$
$-4\frac{3}{3} = 2\frac{1}{7}$

2. $9\frac{1}{5}$
$-8\frac{8}{10}$

3. $1\frac{1}{2}$
$+6\frac{3}{4}$

4. $5\frac{5}{6}$
$-2\frac{7}{12}$

5. $2\frac{5}{8}$
$+2\frac{1}{4}$

6. $7\frac{2}{3}$
$+6\frac{3}{4}$

7. $8\frac{1}{5} - 6\frac{3}{10}$

8. $4\frac{1}{5} - 2\frac{1}{2}$

9. $2\frac{1}{3} + 1\frac{1}{6} + 4\frac{1}{2}$

10. $5\frac{3}{8} + 3\frac{1}{4} + 1\frac{1}{2}$

Identify each angle. Write *acute, right, obtuse, reflex,* or *straight.*

11. 290° angle

12. 37° angle

13. 135° angle

14. 180° angle

15. 90° angle

16. 75° angle

Complete each pattern. Note: There may be more than one operation per pattern set.

17. 5, 7, 11, 13, ▥, ▥, 23

18. ▥, ▥, 4.6, 3.6, 2.6, ▥, ▥

19. 54, 59, 57, ▥, 60, ▥, ▥, ▥

20. 2.9, 3.4, 3.9, ▥, 4.9, ▥, ▥

21. 50, ▥, 34, 22, 18, ▥, ▥, −10

Write all of your answers on a separate sheet of paper.

Simplify the fractions.

22. $\frac{4}{14}$ **23.** $\frac{11}{121}$ **24.** $\frac{14}{6}$ **25.** $\frac{70}{100}$ **26.** $\frac{8}{48}$ **27.** $\frac{3}{18}$

28. $\frac{4}{6}$ **29.** $\frac{6}{1}$ **30.** $\frac{9}{12}$ **31.** $\frac{404}{808}$ **32.** $\frac{14}{16}$ **33.** $\frac{36}{22}$

Solve.

34. $\begin{array}{r} 563 \\ * \ 14 \end{array}$ **35.** $\begin{array}{r} 51 \\ * \ 63 \end{array}$ **36.** $\begin{array}{r} 642 \\ * \ 53 \end{array}$ **37.** $\begin{array}{r} 58{,}225 \\ + \ 16{,}745 \end{array}$

38. $\begin{array}{r} 10{,}345 \\ + \ 4{,}389 \end{array}$ **39.** $\begin{array}{r} 155{,}000 \\ + \ 34{,}500 \end{array}$ **40.** $\begin{array}{r} 899 \\ - \ 76 \end{array}$ **41.** $\begin{array}{r} 440 \\ - \ 105 \end{array}$

Answer the following.

> Radius $= \frac{1}{2} *$ Diameter
> Circumference $= \pi *$ Diameter
> Area $= \pi *$ Radius^2

42. Find the radius of the circle.

43. Find the circumference.

44. Find the area.

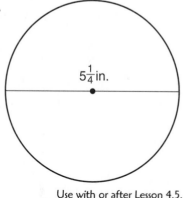

$5\frac{1}{4}$ in.

Use with or after Lesson 4.5.

Practice Set 30

SRB
54 85
216

Write all of your answers on a separate sheet of paper.

Multiply. Write the answer in simplest form.

1. $\frac{4}{5} * \frac{1}{2}$

2. $\frac{3}{8} * \frac{1}{6}$

3. $6 * \frac{3}{10}$

4. $\frac{7}{9} * \frac{1}{6}$

5. $\frac{1}{3} * \frac{1}{3}$

6. $4 * \frac{1}{8}$

7. $\frac{4}{7} * \frac{1}{4}$

8. $\frac{7}{15} * \frac{1}{2}$

Round to the nearest thousandth.

9. 8.2758

10. 10.0756

11. 3.7907

12. 42.9374

13. 0.2898

14. Is point (29,43) above, below, or on the line through points *A* and *B*?

15. Is point (50,30) above, below, or on the line through points *A* and *B*?

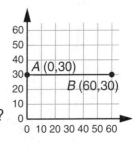

16. Is point (55,16) to the left of, to the right of, or on the line through points *A* and *B*?

17. Is point (35,35) to the left of, to the right of, or on the line through points *A* and *B*?

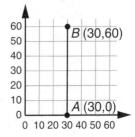

SRB
54 86
214

Write all of your answers on a separate sheet of paper.

Multiply.

1. $2\frac{1}{3} * \frac{1}{5}$

2. $3\frac{1}{6} * 7$

3. $4\frac{2}{3} * 2\frac{1}{3}$

4. $5\frac{1}{2} * 3\frac{3}{8}$

5. $6\frac{5}{6} * 3\frac{1}{3}$

6. $2\frac{3}{4} * 7\frac{1}{2}$

Divide. Round to the nearest hundredth.

7. 92 / 7

8. 55 / 6

9. 128 / 9

10. 89 / 4

11. 100 / 18

12. 155 / 12

Measure each angle to the nearest degree.

13.

14.

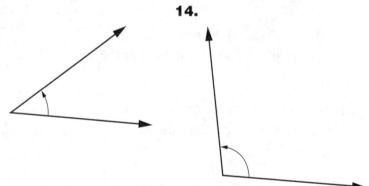

SRB
84 223

Write all of your answers on a separate sheet of paper.

Complete the number lines.

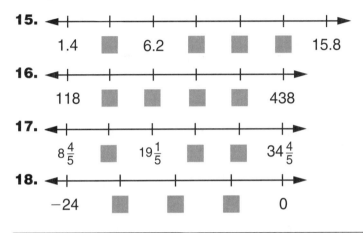

15. 1.4 ■ 6.2 ■ ■ ■ 15.8

16. 118 ■ ■ ■ ■ 438

17. $8\frac{4}{5}$ ■ $19\frac{1}{5}$ ■ ■ $34\frac{4}{5}$

18. −24 ■ ■ ■ 0

Write >, <, or = to make each sentence true.

19. 210.5 ■ 3,376 / 16

20. 72 + 129 ■ 5 ∗ 39

21. 25% of 356 ■ 115 ∗ $\frac{7}{2}$

22. 3,144 − 1,938 ■ 35^2

Write in standard notation.

23. $\sqrt{9}$ **24.** $\sqrt{144}$ **25.** $\sqrt{81}$

26. $\sqrt{25}$ **27.** $\sqrt{121}$ **28.** $\sqrt{49}$

Solve.

29. $\frac{1}{3}$ of 51   **30.** $\frac{2}{3}$ of 84   **31.** $\frac{2}{7}$ of 91

32. $\frac{5}{8}$ of 240   **33.** $\frac{2}{7}$ of 98   **34.** $\frac{7}{11}$ of 143

Write all of your answers on a separate sheet of paper.

Write the missing numbers for the table.

1.

Fraction	Decimal	Percent
■	■	58%
$\frac{6}{18}$	■	■
■	0.5	■
■	0.32	■
$\frac{7}{8}$	■	■
■	■	8%

Evaluate the following algebraic expressions for
$c = 9.3$ and $d = 20$.

2. $c + 1$ **3.** $c - 1.5$ **4.** $c / 3$

5. $c + 10.6$ **6.** $c * 4.6$ **7.** $15 - c$

8. $3d - 1$ **9.** $2d + 6.5$ **10.** $d + d$

11. $200 / d$ **12.** $d - (3 * 2)$ **13.** d^3

Compare. Write < or >.

14. $\frac{1}{7}$ ■ $\frac{1}{6}$ **15.** $\frac{3}{8}$ ■ $\frac{8}{3}$

16. $\frac{2}{4}$ ■ $\frac{2}{12}$ **17.** $\frac{2}{11}$ ■ $\frac{5}{50}$

18. $\frac{7}{10}$ ■ $\frac{12}{25}$ **19.** $\frac{1}{9}$ ■ $\frac{2}{24}$

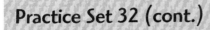
Write all of your answers on a separate sheet of paper.

Write the missing numbers for the table.

20.

Product	Exponential Notation	Standard Notation
■	9^3	■
■	$12^■$	144
■	10^6	■
$\frac{1}{10} * \frac{1}{10} * \frac{1}{10} * \frac{1}{10}$	$10^■$	■

Solve.

21. $a = 7 - 14$ 　　　　**22.** $32 - 66 = b$

23. $4 - 18 = c$ 　　　　**24.** $39 - 47 = d$

25. $-15 - 73 = e$ 　　　**26.** $-900 + 30 = f$

27. $g = 29 - 600$ 　　　**28.** $h = 230 - 35$

29. $45 - 92 = i$ 　　　　**30.** $45 - 39 = j$

31. $70 - 30 = k$ 　　　　**32.** $50 - 80 = l$

33. $2 - 18 = m$ 　　　　**34.** $12 - 77 = n$

Complete the number lines.

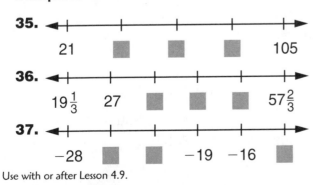

35.

21 　■　■　■　105

36.

$19\frac{1}{3}$　27　■　■　■　$57\frac{2}{3}$

37.

-28　■　■　-19　-16　■

Use with or after Lesson 4.9.

51

Write all of your answers on a separate sheet of paper.

The fourth, fifth, and sixth grades at Apple Valley Elementary sell magazine subscriptions to raise money for field trips.

Magazine Subscription Sales	
Grade	Number of Subscriptions Sold
Fourth	42
Fifth	36
Sixth	72

1. How many magazine subscriptions have been sold in all?
2. What percent has been sold by
   a. the fourth grade
   b. the fifth grade
   c. the sixth grade
3. Make a circle graph of the data.

Complete.

4. $5 * 10^4 = \blacksquare$
5. $5^\blacksquare = 25$
6. $80,000,000 = \blacksquare * 10^7$
7. $3^4 = 8.1 * 10^\blacksquare$
8. $6.4 * 10^\blacksquare = 64,000$
9. $45 * 10^{-4} = \blacksquare$
10. $3.14 * 10^\blacksquare = 314,000,000,000$
11. $6 * 10^\blacksquare = 0.0006$
12. $8.94 * 10^7 = \blacksquare$
13. $943 * 10^{-9} = \blacksquare$

Round 74,082,729,253 to the nearest

14. million
15. ten thousand
16. hundred thousand
17. billion

Write all of your answers on a separate sheet of paper.

Solve.

18. $26\overline{)416}$

19. $\begin{array}{r} 736 \\ * 25 \end{array}$

20. $45\overline{)3,105}$

21. $\begin{array}{r} 11,953 \\ - 10,635 \end{array}$

22. $24\overline{)2,496}$

23. $\begin{array}{r} 118 \\ * 7 \end{array}$

24. $\begin{array}{r} 523 \\ - 153 \end{array}$

25. $\begin{array}{r} 5,835 \\ - 5,823 \end{array}$

26. $\begin{array}{r} 1291 \\ + 412 \end{array}$

27. $\begin{array}{r} 85,431 \\ + 56,432 \end{array}$

28. $(145 \div 5) * 40$

29. $165 - (16 * 9)$

30. $25 * 25 * 18$

31. The temperature at noon was 33°C. The highest temperature that day was 5°C warmer; the lowest was 6°C cooler. What was the temperature range that day?

32. The first temperature reading was 37°F. The second reading showed that the temperature had dropped 13°F. The third reading showed another 13-degree drop. What's the temperature at the third reading?

Complete the "What's My Rule?" tables.

33.

Rule	in	out
in = out $* \frac{5}{8}$	$\frac{5}{40}$ or $\frac{1}{8}$	$\frac{1}{5}$
		$\frac{1}{4}$
		80
	$\frac{15}{32}$	
		$\frac{1}{3}$

34.

Rule	in	out
	786	79
	638	−69
		18
	1,034	
	210	−497

Write all of your answers on a separate sheet of paper.

The Perfect Look Boutique is having a sale. These signs are posted in the store.

Jeans
$5 off

Sweaters
20% off

T-shirts
$11 each

BOOTS
10% off

Raincoats
25% off

1. What is the discount on a sweater that regularly costs $25?

2. What is the sale price of a raincoat that regularly costs $84?

3. What would be the cost of 2 pairs of jeans that regularly cost $30 each?

4. Brittany wants to buy a pair of boots that regularly cost $70 and a sweater that regularly costs $30. What is the total cost, excluding tax?

5. Carleen buys 2 t-shirts and a sweater that regularly costs $40. What is the total cost of her purchases, excluding tax?

Solve the pan-balance problems.

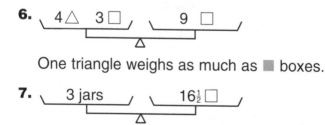

6. 4△ 3☐   9 ☐

One triangle weighs as much as ■ boxes.

7. 3 jars   16½ ☐

One jar weighs as much as ■ boxes.

Write all of your answers on a separate sheet of paper.

Answer the questions about the figures below.

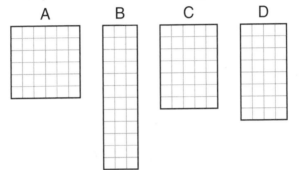

A B C D

8. Which figure has an area of 36 square units and a perimeter of 24 units?

9. Which figure has the largest perimeter, and what is it?

10. Which two figures have the same area?

Write <, >, or = to make the number sentences true.

11. $11.8 \blacksquare \frac{1}{5} * 60$

12. $\frac{4}{6} * 48 \blacksquare 32\%$ of 100

13. $\frac{8}{10} \blacksquare 0.5 * 3$

14. $0.78 \blacksquare 78 * 10^{-3}$

15. $6,586 \blacksquare 70 * 90$

16. $\frac{1}{2} * 0.5 \blacksquare 25 * 10^{-2}$

Solve.

17. $10^5 * 10^8 = \blacksquare$

18. $10^{\blacksquare} = 10^6 * 10^{-3}$

19. $9.8 * 10^3 = \blacksquare$

20. $90,000 = 9 * 10^{\blacksquare}$

21. $A = (3^3 * 26) / 2^3$

22. $1.3 * 10^5 / B = 2$

23. $C = (8.7 + 3.8) * 5$

24. $715 + (100 * 2.94) = D$

25. $7.2 * 10^4 = \blacksquare$

26. $802 + (1,000 * 8.1) = F$

27. $6.3 * 10^5 = \blacksquare$

28. $10^{\blacksquare} = 10^{-2} * 10^{-1}$

Practice Set 35

Write all of your answers on a separate sheet of paper.

Use your full-circle protractor to measure each angle.

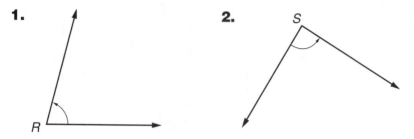

1.

R

2.

S

Tell whether each angle appears to be *acute, right, obtuse, straight,* or *reflex.*

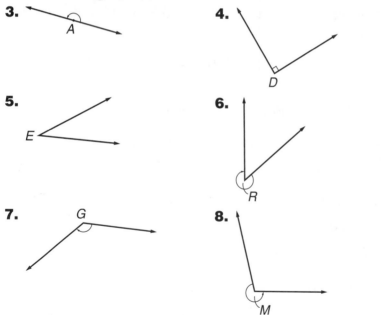

3.

A

4.

D

5.

E

6.

R

7.

G

8.

M

Answer the following question.

9. If the long side is 6.9 cm and the short side is 2.4 cm, what is the perimeter?

Use with or after Lesson 5.1.

Write all of your answers on a separate sheet of paper.

10. Use the clues to complete the puzzle.

▬ ▬ ▬, ▬ ▬ ▬, ▬ ▬ ▬, ▬ ▬ ▬

- Find 10% of 40. Double the result and write it in the thousands place.

- Subtract 6 from the number in the thousands place. Write the answer in the hundred-billions place.

- Find 16 ∗ 3. Reverse the digits in the result and divide by 42. Write the result in the millions place.

- Add 5 to the digit in the hundred-billions place. Divide by 7 and write the result in the hundred-thousands place.

- Write $\frac{28}{7}$ as a whole number in the hundred-millions place.

- Find 35% of 20. Write the result in the ten-millions place.

- Subtract 1 from the number in the hundred-millions place. Write the result in the ten-billions place.

- Find $\frac{8}{9}$ of 108. Divide by 12 and write the result in the billions place.

- Find the sum of all the digits in the chart so far. Divide the result by 7 and write the answer in the hundreds place.

- Write 0 in the remaining places less than billions.

11. Write the number in words.

Practice Set 36

Write all of your answers on a separate sheet of paper.

Write the measure of each angle. Do not use a protractor.

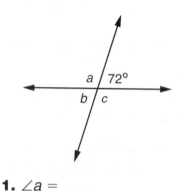

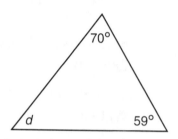

1. ∠a = _____   **2.** ∠b = _____

3. ∠c = _____   **4.** ∠d = _____

Solve.

5.   13
    * 18

6.   28,681
    + 9,478

7. $78\overline{)3{,}734}$

8. A school ordered 145 math books. The books were shipped in boxes that held 8 books each. How many boxes did the school receive?

Write the numbers in order from least to greatest.

9. 3.48, $3\frac{4}{8}$, 4.8, 3.75, $4\frac{2}{5}$, 4.41

10. $4\frac{1}{2}$, 4.75, 2, $3\frac{1}{4}$, 4.8, $4\frac{7}{8}$

11. 0.10, $\frac{1}{1{,}000}$, 0.01, 1.11, $1\frac{1}{10}$, 1.01

12. 8.3, $9\frac{1}{6}$, $8\frac{1}{3}$, 11.01, $9\frac{7}{16}$, 10.8, $10\frac{4}{6}$, $11\frac{1}{5}$

13. $7\frac{5}{8}$, 7.08, 7.88, $7\frac{3}{4}$, 7.8, $7\frac{1}{2}$

14. 6.0, $5\frac{1}{3}$, $6\frac{3}{10}$, $4\frac{1}{5}$, 6.03, 5.33

Write all of your answers on a separate sheet of paper.

Find the number of degrees in a sector of a circle graph to show each percent.

1. 15%   **2.** 30%   **3.** 50%

4. 5%   **5.** 10%   **6.** 75%

Miranda surveyed her classmates about their favorite beverage. She recorded her results in the tally table below.

7. Draw a circle graph to show her results.

Favorite Beverage	
Beverage	**Number of Students**
Milk	ⅢⅢⅢ Ⅲ
Chocolate milk	Ⅲ
Orange juice	Ⅲ Ⅰ
Apple juice	Ⅱ
Soda	Ⅲ Ⅱ

8. Elliot made 3 of 8 shots in the basketball game. What fraction of the shots did he make?

9. What percent of the shots did he miss?

10. At this rate, how many shots would he make if he took 24 shots?

11. Jack has drawn a diagram of shelves he plans to make. Each board is $\frac{7}{8}$ inch thick. What is the width of the shelves?

12. If the boards are all equally spaced, what is the height of each shelf?

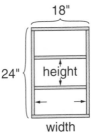

18"
24"
height
width

Practice Set 38

SRB
73
216 224

Write all of your answers on a separate sheet of paper.

Copy the coordinate grid on another sheet of paper.
Plot and label the following points.

> **Example** A (3,2)
>
> The point is plotted on the grid.

1. B (0,4)

2. C (−1,5)

3. D (−2,−4)

4. E (0,0)

5. F (5,1)

6. G (2,−1)

7. H (3,−3)

8. I (−3,3)

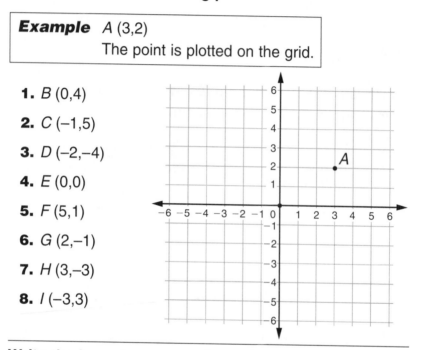

Write the lowest common denominator for each pair of fractions.

9. $\frac{2}{3}, \frac{1}{4}$

10. $\frac{11}{15}, \frac{2}{5}$

11. $\frac{3}{5}, \frac{1}{2}$

12. $\frac{5}{8}, \frac{7}{12}$

13. $\frac{5}{6}, \frac{7}{12}$

14. $\frac{3}{8}, \frac{3}{14}$

Insert parentheses to make each sentence true.

15. $100 - 40 \div 10 = 6$

16. $35 - 3 / 2 + 2 = 8$

17. $5 * 6 + 100 / 5 = 50$

18. $27 * 2 - 4 / 2 = 25$

Use with or after Lesson 5.5.

Write all of your answers on a separate sheet of paper.

Find the distance from 0 to each point and then answer the questions below.

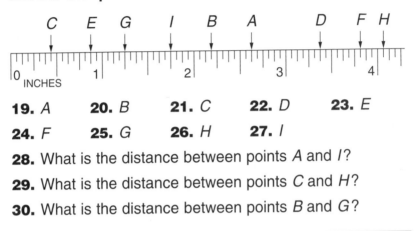

19. A   **20.** B   **21.** C   **22.** D   **23.** E

24. F   **25.** G   **26.** H   **27.** I

28. What is the distance between points A and I?

29. What is the distance between points C and H?

30. What is the distance between points B and G?

---

31. Complete the table.

Product	Exponential Notation	Standard Notation
12 * 12 * 12 * 12 * 12 * 12	▪	▪
▪	$6^{▪}$	7,776
▪	$▪^{8}$	6,561
▪	10^{-11}	▪
19 * 19 * 19	▪	▪

Find the percent of the following.

32. 25% of 280   **33.** 20% of 70   **34.** 30% of 0.4

35. 42% of 250   **36.** 3% of 18   **37.** 76% of 10

38. 11% of 900   **39.** 77% of 800   **40.** 34% of 450

41. 1% of 76   **42.** 10% of 1.3   **43.** 0.1% of 121

Write all of your answers on a separate sheet of paper.

Match the letter of the figure that is congruent with the one given.

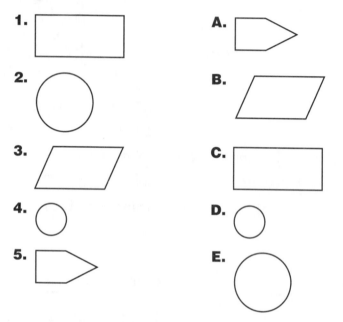

Write an algebraic expression for each word, expression, or situation.

6. 5 more than c

7. h divided by 2

8. 10 times d

9. m subtracted from 1,050

10. Ellen has twice as many tea cups in her collection as Sara. If Sara has t tea cups, how many does Ellen have?

11. Stephan is s meters tall. His brother Eric is 0.2 meters taller. How tall is Eric?

Write all of your answers on a separate sheet of paper.

Solve.

12. 28)448   **13.** 12)780   **14.** 14)4,690   **15.** 278)1,112

16.   634
       − 456

17.   (−33)
       + 735

18.   346
       + 86

19.   512
       * 27

20. 5)1,185   **21.**   40.97
                        − 16.82

22.   4.4
       − 3.9

23.   7.1
       * 6.3

24.   95.235   **25.** 4)7.45   **26.**   853
       − 37.023   − 563

27. 6,384
       + 364

28.   465,891,000
       − 312,747,000

29.   72.94
       + 13.97

30.   6.7
       * 8.1

Suppose you spin the base of the spinner 1,440 times.

31. How many times would you
expect it to land on Part A?

32. How many times would you
expect it to land on Part B?

33. How many times would you
expect it to land on Part C?

34. How many times would you
expect it NOT to land on Part B?

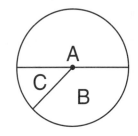

Write all of your answers on a separate sheet of paper.

Find the measure of each angle without using a protractor.

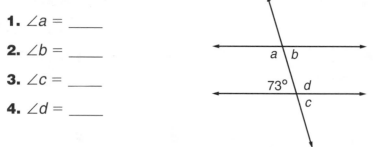

1. $\angle a =$ _____

2. $\angle b =$ _____

3. $\angle c =$ _____

4. $\angle d =$ _____

Find the greatest common factor for each pair of numbers.

5. 6, 9   **6.** 4, 20   **7.** 9, 10

8. 16, 24   **9.** 9, 12   **10.** 8, 18

Write the coordinates for each point.

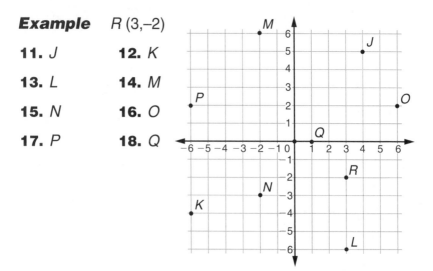

Example $R\,(3,-2)$

11. J **12.** K

13. L **14.** M

15. N **16.** O

17. P **18.** Q

Use with or after Lesson 5.9.

Write all of your answers on a separate sheet of paper.

Figure *LMPN* is a parallelogram. Find the measure of each angle without using a protractor.

1. ∠*r* = _____

2. ∠*s* = _____

3. ∠*t* = _____

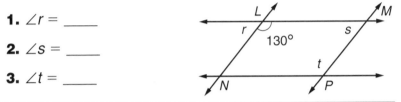

The figure *EFGH* is a rectangle.

4. What is the measure of ∠*E*?

5. What is the length of $\overline{EF}$?

6. What is the length of $\overline{FG}$?

7. What is the perimeter of rectangle *EFGH*?

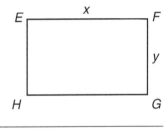

Use the graph to answer the questions below.

At a marathon, Ariana runs at a pace of 6 miles per hour. Glenn walks at a brisk pace that is slightly slower than Ariana's speed.

8. What is Glenn's walking pace?

9. After 3 hours, how much farther has Ariana gone?

10. How much longer will it take Glenn to walk 24 miles than Ariana to run 24 miles?

11. How far behind Ariana is Glenn after 7 hours?

12. Do you think this graph is realistic? Why or why not?

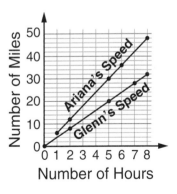

Write all of your answers on a separate sheet of paper.

Answer the following:

13. What is the name of the polygon?

14. If the perimeter is 4.48 cm, what is the length of each side?

Write each in standard notation.

15. fourteen and four-fifths

16. seven hundred eighty-eight trillion, three hundred billion, forty-three million

17. thirty-seven and four hundred eighty-nine thousandths

18. sixteen trillion, two hundred sixty billion, five hundred million

---

Write the words for the following numbers:

19. 5,798,232,026,590

20. 684.948

21. $23\frac{7}{8}$

22. 55.927

Write each fraction as a decimal and a percent.
(Hint: It may help to copy and then fill out the tables.)

23.

Fraction	$\frac{4}{5}$	$\frac{5}{9}$	$\frac{2}{5}$	$\frac{7}{10}$	$\frac{30}{42}$	$\frac{7}{12}$	$5\frac{1}{16}$
Decimal	■	■	■	■	■	■	■
Percent	■	■	■	■	■	■	■

24.

Fraction	$6\frac{3}{4}$	$2\frac{1}{8}$	$\frac{9}{10}$	$\frac{1}{2}$	$\frac{19}{20}$	$4\frac{1}{4}$	$16\frac{3}{5}$
Decimal	■	■	■	■	■	■	■
Percent	■	■	■	■	■	■	■

Use with or after Lesson 5.10.

Write all of your answers on a separate sheet of paper.

Find the reciprocal of each number.

1. $\frac{4}{5}$

2. $\frac{7}{12}$

3. 5

4. $\frac{3}{7}$

5. $1\frac{1}{2}$

6. 9

7. $4\frac{2}{3}$

8. $7\frac{3}{5}$

Multiply. Write your answers in simplest form.

9. $5 * \frac{1}{5}$

10. $6 * \frac{2}{3}$

11. $\frac{3}{7} * \frac{2}{5}$

12. $1\frac{1}{2} * 5$

13. $2\frac{1}{8} * 5\frac{1}{3}$

14. $4\frac{1}{5} * \frac{5}{7}$

Divide. Round to the nearest hundredth.

15. 543 / 9

16. 265 / 6

17. 921 / 7

18. 497 / 3

19. 251 / 12

20. 801 / 27

Use digits to write the following numbers:

21. eighty-two billion, six hundred thirty-three million

22. seventy-two million, one hundred sixteen thousand, four hundred forty-nine

23. seven and eight-tenths

24. twelve and ninety-three hundredths

Write all of your answers on a separate sheet of paper.

25. Write the missing numbers for the table.

Fraction	Percent	Decimal
$\frac{7}{8}$	■	■
■	■	0.99
■	38%	■
■	■	2.03

$$0.875$$
$$8\overline{)70}$$
$$-64$$
$$\overline{60}$$
$$-56$$
$$\overline{40}$$
$$-40$$
$$\overline{0}$$

Solve.

Christie bought two pairs of sandals that were $12.99 each. Adam bought three pairs of sandals. His total came to $24.57.

26. Who paid more money overall?

27. Who got the better deal per pair of shoes? Explain.

John bought a tool set that was 25% off. The original price was $48.

28. How much did he pay for the tool set?

29. How much money did John save?

30. LeAnn paid $\frac{1}{4}$ of the price that Richard paid for 10 pencils. LeAnn paid $2 for the pencils. How much did Richard pay for one pencil?

31. Use the digits to write the largest number less than 5.

6, 4, 2, 0, 9

Use with or after Lesson 6.1.

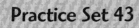
Write all of your answers on a separate sheet of paper.

Divide. Show your work. Write each answer in simplest form.

> **Example** $\frac{4}{5} \div \frac{3}{10}$
>
> $\frac{4}{5} * \frac{10}{3} = \frac{40}{15}$
>
> **Answer:** $2\frac{10}{15}$ or $2\frac{2}{3}$

1. $\frac{1}{3} \div \frac{1}{2}$ **2.** $\frac{3}{5} \div \frac{3}{10}$

3. $\frac{7}{8} \div \frac{4}{5}$ **4.** $\frac{4}{9} \div \frac{4}{9}$

5. $6 \div \frac{1}{5}$ **6.** $\frac{1}{2} \div \frac{3}{8}$

7. $2\frac{1}{5} \div \frac{1}{10}$ **8.** $9 \div \frac{1}{3}$

9. $3\frac{1}{2} \div \frac{1}{12}$ **10.** $5\frac{1}{3} \div \frac{8}{5}$

11. $3 \div \frac{3}{8}$ **12.** $4\frac{1}{6} \div \frac{5}{8}$

13. $\frac{2}{5} \div \frac{1}{2}$ **14.** $4\frac{3}{8} \div \frac{2}{7}$

Solve.

15. 2,247   **16.** 1,309   **17.**   837   **18.** $18\overline{)556}$
     $-\,1,894$ $+\,782$ $-\,784$

19. 8,926   **20.**   41   **21.** $37\overline{)6,298}$ **22.** 6,473
     $-\,2,481$ $*\,83$ $-\,5,498$

23. 723   **24.** 31,955   **25.** 904   **26.** 16,980
      $*\,3$ $+\,19,079$ $*\,61$ $+\,14,062$

Write all of your answers on a separate sheet of paper.

Complete each pattern. Then describe the pattern.

27. 12, 19, 26, ■, 40, ■, ■, 61

28. 142, 71, 35.5, ■, 8.875, ■, 2.21875

29. 0, 4; ■, 5; ■, 6; 0, ■; 0, 8

30. ■, 0, 1.4, ■, ■, 5.6, ■, 8.4

Copy the coordinate graph. Plot the points shown and write each letter next to the given ordered pair. Connect the points in alphabetical order.

31. *A:* (−1,−9)   **32.** *G:* (0,−3)   **33.** *M:* (6,7)

34. *O:* (2,5)   **35.** *D:* (3,−1)   **36.** *B:* (−1,−6)

37. *U:* (−5,3)   **38.** *K:* (3,1)   **39.** *L:* (4,4)

40. *N:* (3,6)   **41.** *C:* (2,−4)   **42.** *T:* (−5,5)

43. *J:* (−1,0)   **44.** *V:* (−3,1)   **45.** *Q:* (−2,5)

46. *E:* (4,1)

47. *F:* (2,−1)

48. *S:* (−6,7)

49. *I:* (−1,−2)

50. *P:* (0,7)

51. *R:* (−3,6)

52. *H:* (−1,−4)

53. *W:* (−1,0)

Write all of your answers on a separate sheet of paper.

Subtract.

1. $16 - (-14)$ **2.** $-125 - 87$

3. $3.5 - (-6.7)$ **4.** $-5.7 - (-8.9)$

5. $-4\frac{1}{2} - (-6\frac{1}{2})$ **6.** $12.83 - (-6.59)$

7. $257 - (-183)$ **8.** $5 - (-4\frac{2}{3})$

9. $15.8 - (-3.3)$ **10.** $3\frac{5}{16} - (-1\frac{5}{8})$

Write the numbers in exponential notation.

11. $10 * 10 * 10$

12. $14 * 14 * 14 * 14 * 14$

13. $2 * 2$

14. $7 * 7 * 7 * 7$

15. $143 * 143 * 143 * 143 * 143 * 143 * 143$

16. $10{,}416 * 10{,}416 * 10{,}416$

Add or subtract. Write all answers greater than 1 as mixed numbers. Write all answers in simplest form.

17. $\frac{2}{7} + \frac{1}{4}$ **18.** $\frac{4}{9} + \frac{2}{3}$ **19.** $\frac{1}{2} - \frac{14}{30}$

20. $\frac{6}{7} - \frac{1}{14}$ **21.** $\frac{9}{4} + \frac{1}{6}$ **22.** $\frac{5}{6} - \frac{2}{3}$

23. $\frac{1}{24} + \frac{2}{3}$ **24.** $\frac{15}{16} + \frac{3}{4}$ **25.** $\frac{9}{10} - \frac{2}{5}$

26. $\frac{11}{36} + \frac{1}{2}$ **27.** $\frac{7}{12} - \frac{1}{2}$ **28.** $\frac{17}{20} - \frac{4}{5}$

29. $\frac{13}{18} + \frac{1}{9}$ **30.** $\frac{3}{5} + \frac{1}{10}$ **31.** $\frac{8}{9} - \frac{1}{3}$

Practice Set 45

SRB
95 222
227 228

Write all of your answers on a separate sheet of paper.

Solve.

1. $-7 * -5$ **2.** $56 / (-8)$

3. $(-180) / 10$ **4.** $(-9) * 6$

5. $(-63) \div (-9)$ **6.** $(-3) * 4 * (-8)$

7. $(23 - 3) / (-5)$ **8.** $60 / (-5)$

9. $(-6) * (8 + 5)$ **10.** $(-2 - 12) / 2$

Evaluate each algebraic expression for $a = 5$ and $f = 1.2$.

11. $6 * a$ **12.** $9 - f$ **13.** $30 / a$

14. $7 + f$ **15.** $50 - a$ **16.** $10f$

17. $2(f + 0.8)$ **18.** $a / 5$ **19.** $8 + 2a$

Write an algebraic expression for each phrase.

20. A number t increased by 35

21. The sum of a number m and 105

22. A number s decreased by 19

23. The total when a number s is added to 31

24. 50 decreased by a number x

25. A number r minus 7

       Use with or after Lesson 6.4.

Write all of your answers on a separate sheet of paper.

Complete the following tables.

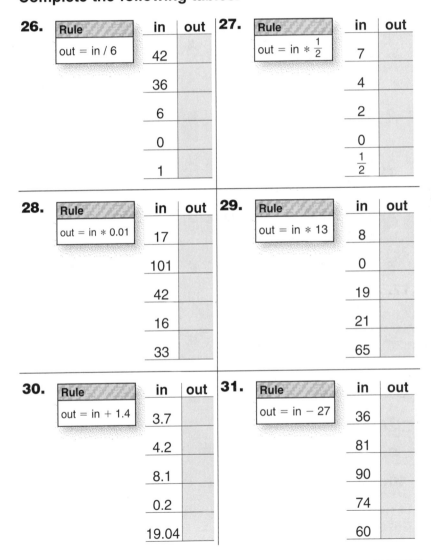

26.

Rule	in	out
out = in / 6	42	
	36	
	6	
	0	
	1	

27.

Rule	in	out
out = in * $\frac{1}{2}$	7	
	4	
	2	
	0	
	$\frac{1}{2}$	

28.

Rule	in	out
out = in * 0.01	17	
	101	
	42	
	16	
	33	

29.

Rule	in	out
out = in * 13	8	
	0	
	19	
	21	
	65	

30.

Rule	in	out
out = in + 1.4	3.7	
	4.2	
	8.1	
	0.2	
	19.04	

31.

Rule	in	out
out = in − 27	36	
	81	
	90	
	74	
	60	

Find the mean for the following groups of numbers.

32. 4, 9, 8, 7, 1, 0, 9

33. 14, 19, 24, 16, 31, 29, 18

Write all of your answers on a separate sheet of paper.

Match each number sentence with a property. Write the letter of the number sentence.

1. Distributive Property of Multiplication over Addition

A. $7(6.2 - 5.1) =$ $7(6.2) - 7(5.1)$

2. Commutative Property of Addition

B. $\frac{1}{3}(9 + 5) = \frac{1}{3}(9) + \frac{1}{3}(5)$

3. Associative Property of Multiplication

C. $(15 - 6) + 8 =$ $8 + (15 - 6)$

4. Commutative Property of Multiplication

D. $3 * 1 = 3$

5. Distributive Property of Multiplication over Subtraction

E. $3 * (2 * 5) = (3 * 2) * 5$

6. Identity Property for Multiplication

F. $25 * 150 = 150 * 25$

Compare. Write < , >, or =.

7. $-24 + (-5)$ ■ $162 - 70$ **8.** $-5 - 4$ ■ 0

9. $-100 - 43$ ■ $-200 + 57$

10. $9.2 - (-6.1)$ ■ $8.2 + 4.5$

11. -153 ■ $(-6) * (-8) * (-3)$

12. $425 * 0$ ■ $-260 + 260$

13. $(-5) * (-6)$ ■ $(4.6) * (-3.1)$

14. $-529 + 60$ ■ $-500 - 37$

Write all of your answers on a separate sheet of paper.

Evaluate each expression.

1. $17 + 3 * 2 - 1$

2. $3^2 + 7(10 - 5)$

3. $(5.1 + 9.4) * 3 + 2$

4. $(4 + 16) / 10 + 9$

5. $100 - 62 * 3 + 75$

6. $\frac{3}{5} * \frac{1}{3} + \frac{1}{10} * 2$

7. Use the clues to complete the place-value puzzle.

___ . ___ ___ ___ ___

- Write 75% of 12 in the hundredths place.
- Find $\frac{1}{25}$ of 115. Add 1.4 and write the result in the thousandths place.
- Take $\frac{4}{9}$ of the number in the hundredths place. Write the result in the ten-thousandths place.
- Multiply $8 * 34$. Subtract 265 and write the result in the ones place.
- Subtract 200% of 0.5 from the number in the thousandths place. Write the result in the tenths place.

Solve.

8.   736
     + 264

9.   253
      + 86

10.   365
      − 375

11. 253
      − 27

12. 364
      − 94

13. 7,437
      + 983

14. 6,345
      + 1,052

15.   2,852
      − 1,865

Write all of your answers on a separate sheet of paper.

Convert each fraction into a whole number or mixed number.

16. $\frac{14}{3}$ **17.** $\frac{9}{1}$ **18.** $\frac{23}{8}$ **19.** $\frac{10}{2}$

20. $\frac{18}{5}$ **21.** $\frac{26}{6}$ **22.** $\frac{30}{4}$ **23.** $\frac{25}{7}$

24. $\frac{20}{10}$ **25.** $\frac{27}{3}$ **26.** $\frac{98}{5}$ **27.** $\frac{19}{4}$

Answer each question. You can use the number line to help you.

28. What is $\frac{1}{4}$ of 4?   **29.** What is $\frac{1}{2}$ of $\frac{1}{2}$?

30. What is $\frac{1}{2}$ of $\frac{1}{4}$?   **31.** What is $\frac{1}{4}$ of 1?

32. What is $\frac{1}{2}$ of 3?   **33.** What is $\frac{1}{8}$ of 2?

34. What is $\frac{3}{4}$ of 4?   **35.** What is $\frac{5}{8}$ of 2?

36. What is $\frac{3}{8}$ of 4?   **37.** What is $\frac{3}{4}$ of 3?

38. What is $\frac{2}{3}$ of 3?   **39.** What is $\frac{1}{2}$ of $\frac{3}{4}$?

Order the fractions from least to greatest.

40. $\frac{1}{6}, \frac{1}{9}, \frac{1}{12}, \frac{1}{15}$

41. $\frac{2}{7}, \frac{4}{13}, \frac{5}{6}, \frac{6}{13}$

42. $\frac{2}{3}, \frac{1}{6}, \frac{3}{4}, \frac{11}{12}$

43. $\frac{7}{12}, \frac{1}{4}, \frac{7}{8}, \frac{5}{6}$

44. $\frac{3}{16}, \frac{1}{8}, \frac{3}{4}, \frac{1}{2}$

45. $\frac{4}{5}, \frac{3}{10}, \frac{1}{2}, \frac{1}{15}$

Write all of your answers on a separate sheet of paper.

Write *true* or *false* for each number sentence.

1. $9 * 8 = 72$

2. $100 - 36 = 65$

3. $6 * 4 - 3 = 6$

4. $126 / 7 = 20$

5. $125 - 150 / 50 = 122$

6. $90 - 45 \leq 45$

7. $80 / (4 + 4) \geq 12$

8. $12 * 12 \neq 135$

9. $40 + (6 * 2) = 48$

10. $92 / 6 + 7 < 50$

Write the letter of the line plot that makes sense with the survey question.

```
            X                        X
            X                        X
    X   X   X                        X
    X   X   X                        X   X
    X   X   X                X   X   X   X   X
    X   X   X   X            X   X   X   X   X
X   X   X   X   X            X   X   X   X   X
+---+---+---+---+           +---+---+---+---+
6   7   8   9   10          0   1   2   3   4
```

Line Plot A   **Line Plot B**

11. How many hours do you sleep each night?

12. How many hours of TV do you watch each day?

Add. Use mental math.

13. $(-1) + 2 + (-11)$

14. $(-17) + (8)$

15. $(-5) + 6 + (-1)$

16. $10 + (-3) + 2$

17. $3 + (-5) + (-6)$

18. $-9 + (-4) + 2$

Practice Set 49

Write all of your answers on a separate sheet of paper.

Find the solution to each equation.

1. $4 + a = 10$

2. $20 + t = 50$

3. $18 = b + 9$

4. $\frac{1}{3} * p = \frac{4}{15}$

5. $25c = 200$

6. $4n = 60$

Estimate. Round to the nearest whole number, the nearest ten, or the nearest hundred before you multiply.

7. $762 * 81$

8. $2.4 * 6.7$

9. $91 * 823$

10. $52.1 * 76.3$

11. $801 * 104$

12. $4.72 * 1.07$

13. $484 * 621$

14. $4.72 * 5.07$

15. $708 * 814$

16. $312 * 847$

17. $907 * 382$

18. $6.09 * 1.49$

19. $3.2002 * 3.2002$

20. $8.01 * 1.24967$

21. $3.132 * 9.17$

22. $1.00769 * 712.514$

23. $6.26 * 7.39$

24. $1618 * 1732$

Divide. Include remainders in your answers where needed.

25. $2{,}158 \div 83 = \blacksquare$

26. $1{,}633 \div 71 = \blacksquare$

27. $42{,}240 \div 352 = \blacksquare$

28. $366{,}450 \div 698 = \blacksquare$

29. $206{,}322 \div 411 = \blacksquare$

30. $576{,}312 \div 814 = \blacksquare$

31. $251 \div 21 \rightarrow \blacksquare$

32. $1{,}410 \div 13 \rightarrow \blacksquare$

33. $7{,}621 \div 63 \rightarrow \blacksquare$

34. $904 \div 204 \rightarrow \blacksquare$

Write all of your answers on a separate sheet of paper.

Solve each pan-balance problem. In each drawing, the two pans are in perfect balance.

1. One cube weighs as much as ■ marbles.

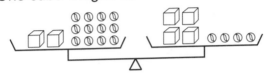

2. One baseball bat weighs as much as ■ balls.

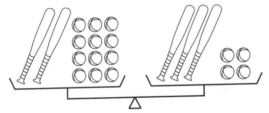

3. One P weighs as much as ■ Q.

| 12 P | 4 P   2 Q |

4. One B weighs as much as ■ G.

| 4 B   6 G | 10 B   3 G |

5. One T weighs as much as ■ S.

| 3 S | 9 T |

6. One L weighs as much as ■ A.

| 6 L   4 A | 3 A   8 L |

Write all of your answers on a separate sheet of paper.

Use the grid to answer the questions below.

Each square in the grid below represents a city block. There are 8 blocks in a mile, so each side of each block is $\frac{1}{8}$ mile long.

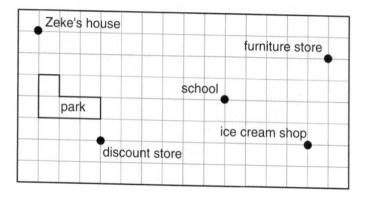

7. What is the shortest distance between Zeke's house and school?

8. If Zeke goes to the ice cream shop before going home from school, how far will he have walked?

9. After leaving the house, Zeke's mom dropped Zeke and his brother at the park, then drove to the discount store and the furniture store before returning home. What is the shortest distance she could have driven?

10. What is the area of the park, in square miles?

11. What is the area, in square miles, shown on the entire grid map?

Write all of your answers on a separate sheet of paper.

Evaluate each algebraic expression.

1. $3y - 4 = 11$

2. $10 = 2n$

3. $12 = 14 - z$

4. $16 + 7 = m$

5. $16 = p^4$

6. $21 = 7s - 7$

7. $17 * r / 2 = 34$

8. $104 \div q = 13$

9. $7 = 49 / a$

10. $(s \div 3) + 12 = 12$

11. $6 = \frac{36}{b} + 2$

12. $8u - 4 = 44$

13. $8 + 7w = 15$

14. $0 = (104 + 206) * d$

15. $9^2 = x$

16. $\frac{6h}{2} = 27$

17. $44 = 3x + 8$

18. $\frac{96}{y} = 24$

Solve.

19. $\begin{array}{r} 8.47 \\ * 6 \\ \hline \end{array}$

20. $\begin{array}{r} 3.19 \\ * 100 \\ \hline \end{array}$

21. $\begin{array}{r} 4.45 \\ + 6.96 \\ \hline \end{array}$

22. $\begin{array}{r} 2.408 \\ + 7.334 \\ \hline \end{array}$

23. $\begin{array}{r} 9.294 \\ - 6.275 \\ \hline \end{array}$

24. $\begin{array}{r} 7.025 \\ * 8 \\ \hline \end{array}$

25. $\begin{array}{r} 12,645 \\ - 6,792 \\ \hline \end{array}$

26. $\begin{array}{r} 33.25 \\ + 79.87 \\ \hline \end{array}$

27. $\frac{1}{4} + \frac{3}{4} + \frac{5}{6}$

28. $14.812 + 12.265 + 6.408$

29. $\frac{2}{3} * \frac{7}{9}$

30. $5 - (\frac{4}{5} + \frac{2}{3})$

Practice Set 52

SRB
74
224–226

Write all of your answers on a separate sheet of paper.

Match the solution set with the inequality. Write the letter of the solution set.

1. $5 < r$

2. $-\frac{15}{3} \geq s$

3. $4s > 24$

4. $9y \leq 18$

5. $25 - 4 > p$

A. All numbers less than 21

B. All numbers less than or equal to -5

C. All numbers less than or equal to 2

D. All numbers greater than 6

E. All numbers greater than 5

Find the least common multiple for each pair of numbers.

6. 9, 20   **7.** 30, 36   **8.** 7, 10
9. 5, 10   **10.** 12, 16   **11.** 7, 8

Rewrite the number sentences with parentheses to make them correct.

12. $24 - 15 + 7 = 16$ **13.** $24 - 15 + 7 = 2$

14. $15 + 15 * 4 = 75$ **15.** $15 + 15 * 4 = 120$

16. $21 - 12 / 3 * 2 = 13$ **17.** $21 - 12 / 3 * 2 = 34$

18. $17 - 9 + 4 + 3 = 15$ **19.** $17 - 9 + 4 + 3 = 1$

20. $45 / 9 + 6 = 3$ **21.** $45 / 9 + 6 = 11$

Complete.

22. $\frac{1}{3}$ hr $= \frac{\blacksquare}{15}$ hr   **23.** $\frac{1}{2}$ min $= \frac{4}{\blacksquare}$ min

24. $\frac{2}{6}$ hr $= \frac{\blacksquare}{3}$ hr   **25.** $\frac{\blacksquare}{8}$ hr $= \frac{12}{32}$ hr

Use with or after Lesson 6.12.

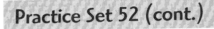
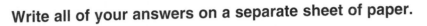
Write all of your answers on a separate sheet of paper.

The town of State College lies in a valley that experiences much precipitation. Use the data in the tables for questions 26–29.

Average Number of Days in State College with at Least 0.01 Inch of Precipitation

Month	Jan.	Feb.	Mar.	Apr.	May	June
Number of Days	18	17	15	14	10	8

Month	July	Aug.	Sept.	Oct.	Nov.	Dec.
Number of Days	9	11	17	20	20	18

26. Use the information about precipitation in State College to make a broken-line graph.

27. Find the mean for the number of days with at least 0.01 inch of precipitation.

28. Find the mode for the number of days State College received at least 0.01 inch of precipitation.

29. Find the median for the graph.

Write *true* or *false* for each number sentence.

30. $(9+3) / 4 = 3$

31. $\frac{9}{(3 + 6)} = 9$

32. $6 - (2 / 4) = 5\frac{1}{2}$

33. $18 + (9 * 4) = 54$

34. $(8 + 7) = 8 + 7$

35. $(6 * 4) - 2 = 20$

36. $6 + \frac{1}{8} = \frac{(6 + 1)}{8}$

37. $4^2 = 2^2 * 4$

38. $4^2 > 2^5$

39. $\frac{(2 + 4)}{3} = 2 + \frac{4}{3}$

40. $(3 + 2) * 12 = 60$

41. $(\frac{6}{3}) + (\frac{8}{3}) = \frac{(6 + 8)}{3}$

Write all of your answers on a separate sheet of paper.

Use the spinners to help you answer questions 1–4.

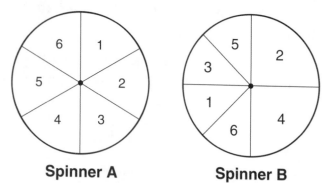

Spinner A   Spinner B

1. Which spinner has outcomes that are equally likely?

2. What is the probability of spinning an even number using Spinner A?

3. What is the probability of spinning an odd number using Spinner B?

4. What is the probability of spinning a number less than 5 using Spinner A?

Find the measure of the missing angles without measuring.

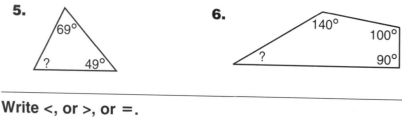

5. 69° ? 49°

6. 140° 100° ? 90°

Write <, or >, or =.

7. 9.4 ■ $\frac{2}{5} * 20$

8. $\frac{7}{8} * 48$ ■ 34% of 150

9. $\frac{7}{10}$ ■ $\frac{4}{5} * \frac{1}{2}$

10. 0.04 ■ $4 * 10^{-1}$

11. 8.39 ■ $34 * \frac{1}{4}$

12. 7.31 ■ $73.1 * 10^{-1}$

Write all of your answers on a separate sheet of paper.

Use this section of a table of random digits to answer questions 1–4.

Let each digit represent the results of a game. Even stands for a win. Odd stands for a loss.

```
0 8 1 0 5 5 9 9 8 7
8 7 1 1 2 2 1 4 7 6
1 4 7 1 3 7 1 1 8 1
```

1. a. How many wins are in the first 10 games?
   b. What percent of the first 10 games are wins?

2. a. How many wins are in 20 games?
   b. What percent of the 20 games are wins?

3. a. How many wins are in 30 games?
   b. What percent of the 30 games are wins?

4. What do you think the percent of wins would be if you had a table of random digits that had 1,000 digits? Explain your answer.

Rewrite the number sentences with parentheses to make them correct.

5. $143 = 7 + 6 * 11$ **6.** $7 + 6 * 11 = 73$

7. $54 - 22 + 17 = 49$ **8.** $15 = 54 - 22 + 17$

9. $46 = 7 * 4 + 18$ **10.** $7 * 4 + 18 = 154$

11. $6 * 2 + 19 * 7 = 145$ **12.** $6 * 2 + 19 * 7 = 882$

Solve.

13. $(-98) + (-25) = y$ **14.** $(+2,355) + (-5,234) = J$

15. $r + (+235) = (-945)$ **16.** $M = (-734) + (-900)$

Write all of your answers on a separate sheet of paper.

Use the tree diagrams below to help you solve the problems. (Copy the blank diagrams on your paper.)

1. Suppose 90 people walked through the maze below. How many people would you expect to end up in Room A? How many people would you expect to end up in Room B?

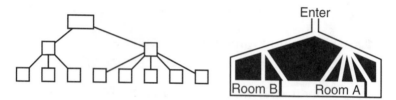

2. Suppose 120 people walked through the maze below. How many people would you expect to end up in Room A? How many people would you expect to end up in Room B?

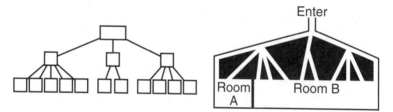

3. Suppose 100 people walked through the maze below. How many people would you expect to end up in Room A? How many people would you expect to end up in Room B?

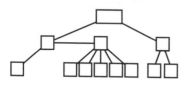

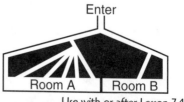

Use with or after Lesson 7.4

Write all of your answers on a separate sheet of paper.

Multiply.

4. $\frac{4}{9} * \frac{1}{6}$ **5.** $\frac{2}{18} * \frac{16}{13}$ **6.** $\frac{7}{9} * \frac{12}{14}$

7. $\frac{8}{20} * \frac{7}{16}$ **8.** $\frac{7}{16} * \frac{9}{10}$ **9.** $\frac{3}{40} * \frac{2}{50}$

10. $\frac{14}{20} * \frac{7}{18}$ **11.** $\frac{46}{12} * \frac{11}{18}$ **12.** $\frac{12}{17} * \frac{21}{12}$

13. $\frac{4}{19} * \frac{3}{8}$ **14.** $\frac{2}{13} * \frac{24}{25}$ **15.** $\frac{0}{1} * \frac{82}{1000}$

16. $4\frac{1}{8} * 3\frac{1}{9}$ **17.** $1\frac{4}{6} * 3\frac{2}{9}$ **18.** $10\frac{3}{5} * 8\frac{7}{15}$

19. $9\frac{10}{17} * 4\frac{3}{9}$ **20.** $3\frac{1}{2} * 5\frac{1}{3}$ **21.** $21\frac{7}{8} * 1\frac{6}{7}$

22. $8\frac{9}{10} * 7\frac{9}{10}$ **23.** $6\frac{2}{3} * 6\frac{2}{3}$ **24.** $12\frac{1}{3} * 8\frac{1}{4}$

Write each number in scientific notation.

25. 4,910,000   **26.** 81,724,691,482,000

27. 862,149,000   **28.** 33,334,041,100

29. 26,710,400   **30.** 2,811,462,700

31. 361,247,098,000   **32.** 320,000,000,000

33. 123,456,789   **34.** 540,000,017

35. 6,565,656   **36.** 56,010

Write the number for each of the following.

37. $8^2 + 6^2$ **38.** 10^{10}

39. $4^3 + 2^4$ **40.** $7^2 / 7^0$

41. $7^2 / 7^1$ **42.** $9^2 + 3^3$

43. $2^4 / 2^2$ **44.** $5^3 / 5^1$

45. $10^2 * 10^2$ **46.** $11^2 - 3^3$

Use with or after Lesson 7.4.

87

Write all of your answers on a separate sheet of paper.

Determine the probability of tossing a coin and achieving the given outcome.

1. heads, heads, heads

2. tails, tails, tails

3. heads, tails, tails

4. tails, heads, tails

5. heads, heads, tails

6. tails, heads

7. tails, tails, heads, heads

8. tails, heads, tails, tails, heads

9. tails, tails, tails, heads, heads, heads

10. heads, heads, heads, heads

Solve the pan-balance problems. Assume that each object weighs the same for every pan balance on this page.

11.

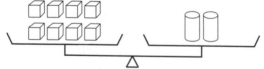

One cylinder weighs as much as ■ blocks.

12.

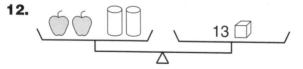

One apple weighs as much as ■ blocks.

Write the greatest common factor for each pair of numbers.

13. 24, 30   **14.** 12, 48   **15.** 20, 50

16. 6, 15   **17.** 18, 25   **18.** 22, 40

Use with or after Lesson 7.5.

Write all of your answers on a separate sheet of paper.

Write each fraction in simplest form.

19. $\frac{4}{2}$ **20.** $\frac{16}{18}$ **21.** $\frac{10}{5}$ **22.** $\frac{12}{24}$ **23.** $\frac{3}{9}$

24. $\frac{2}{20}$ **25.** $\frac{10}{100}$ **26.** $\frac{21}{21}$ **27.** $\frac{18}{20}$ **28.** $\frac{4}{14}$

Find the perimeter and the area of each figure, using the proper formula.

Area = Length * Width
Perimeter = 2 * Length + 2 * Width

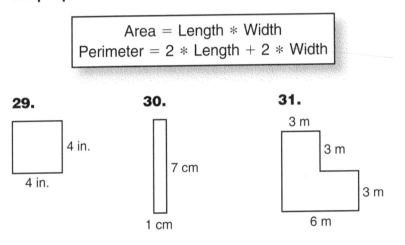

29.

4 in.

4 in.

30.

7 cm

1 cm

31.

3 m

3 m

3 m

6 m

Solve each problem.

32. Andrea drove 500 miles in 10 hours. Find the average number of miles per hour that Andrea drove.

33. Michael paid $45 for a shirt that was on sale. The original price was $78. How much did he save by buying the shirt on sale?

34. Pat wants to make a double batch of cookies. If the original recipe calls for $\frac{3}{4}$ cup of sugar, how much sugar should she use?

Write all of your answers on a separate sheet of paper.

Draw a Venn diagram for each problem. Then answer the question.

Example Twelve students in Ms. DeCola's English class read *Sounder*. Eighteen students read a biography of Michael Jordan. There are 24 students in her class. How many students read both books?

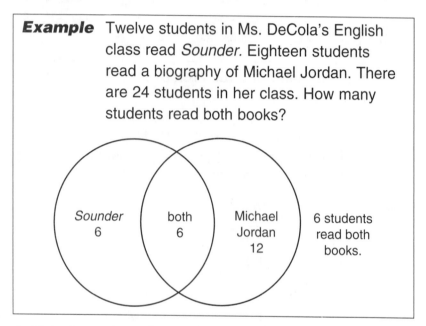

1. Twenty students brought all or part of their lunch from home. Fifteen students in Ms. DeCola's class bought all or part of their lunch from the cafeteria. How many students *brought* part of their lunch and *bought* another part of their lunch?

2. Twenty-two students in Ms. DeCola's class played baseball during the summer. Seventeen students played soccer, and 6 played both baseball and soccer. Twelve students also played tennis. If 4 students played all three sports, 5 students played baseball and tennis, and 2 students played soccer and tennis, how many students only played baseball, soccer, or tennis?

Write all of your answers on a separate sheet of paper.

Match each percent with its equivalent fraction. Write the letter of that fraction.

3. 25%   **a.** $\frac{7}{8}$

4. 12.5%   **b.** $\frac{1}{2}$

5. 60%   **c.** $\frac{9}{12}$

6. 20%   **d.** $\frac{1}{40}$

7. 36%   **e.** $\frac{15}{60}$

8. 75%   **f.** $\frac{9}{25}$

9. 2.5%   **g.** $\frac{7}{10}$

10. 70%   **h.** $\frac{1}{5}$

11. 50%   **i.** $\frac{1}{8}$

12. 87.5%   **j.** $\frac{3}{5}$

Find each missing number.

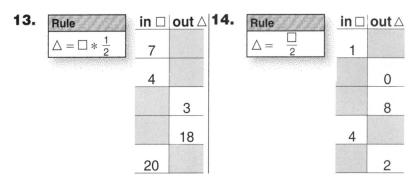

13.

Rule $\triangle = \square * \frac{1}{2}$	in $\square$	out $\triangle$
	7	
	4	
		3
		18
	20	

14.

Rule $\triangle = \frac{\square}{2}$	in $\square$	out $\triangle$
	1	
		0
		8
	4	
		2

Write all of your answers on a separate sheet of paper.

Tell whether each game is fair. Explain your answer. Each game is for one player and uses number cards for the numbers 1–30, shuffled and placed face down.

1. To win you must draw a number divisible by 5.

2. To win you must draw a number less than 16.

3. To win you must draw a number greater than 30.

4. To win you must draw a number less than 60.

Write the reciprocal for each number.

5. $\frac{1}{4}$ **6.** $\frac{5}{16}$ **7.** 38   **8.** $2\frac{3}{4}$

9. $18\frac{1}{2}$ **10.** $\frac{6}{5}$ **11.** $5\frac{1}{3}$ **12.** $9\frac{1}{6}$

Solve each equation.

13. $3 * t = 21$ **14.** $4 = 60 \div a$ **15.** $x + 6 = (-4)$

16. $14 + s = 42$ **17.** $x * 16 = 64$ **18.** $136 \div r = (-8)$

19. $12 = n \div 9$ **20.** $p - 12 = 2$ **21.** $-2 = g - 12$

22. $19 * v = 133$ **23.** $80 = 21 + s$ **24.** $n \div 11 = 6$

25. $w - 18 = 9$ **26.** $0 = 20 * y$ **27.** $12 + e = 21$

28. $41 - x = 44$ **29.** $52 \div x = 4$ **30.** $v * 14 = (-70)$

Write all of your answers on a separate sheet of paper.

Write each number in standard notation.

31. four thousand, seven hundred twelve

32. six thousand, eight hundred forty-six

33. nine thousand, one hundred ninety-six

34. one thousand, seven

35. 9^2 **36.** 4^2 **37.** 8^3 **38.** 3^4

39. 2^6 **40.** 10^9 **41.** 5^3 **42.** 7^3

43. 6^4 **44.** 3^6 **45.** 12^2 **46.** 20^2

47. 10^{-4} **48.** 10^4 **49.** 10^{-1} **50.** 1.3^2

Find the rule and the missing numbers for each table.

51.

Rule	in	out
	4	8
	10	14
		21
	7	
	0	
		13

52.

Rule	in	out
	21	7
	30	10
		3
		12
	9	
	0	

Find the mean for each group of numbers.

53. 4, 9, 1, 12, 7

54. 11, 21, 31, 41, 25

55. 2, 1, 2, 2, 19

56. 46, 50, 41, 39, 52

57. 7, 6, 7, 6, 8

58. 19, 12, 21, 54, 72

Write all of your answers on a separate sheet of paper.

Complete the tables and answer the questions.

1. Bacteria grow 2 mm every four hours.

Hours	1	2	■	4	■	12	13	■	■	■
Millimeters	■	■	$1\frac{1}{2}$	2	$2\frac{1}{2}$	■	■	8	9	$10\frac{1}{2}$

2. If the bacteria kept growing at this rate, how long would they be after 2 days? (Remember: 24 hours = 1 day)

3. Mr. Fikey drove 60 miles in 60 minutes.

Miles	■	■	■	60	71	■	101	109	120	■
Minutes	5	20	45	■	■	94	■	■	■	135

4. How many hours would it take Mr. Fikey to drive 660 miles? (Remember: 1 hour = 60 minutes)

5. 16 ounces = 1 pound

Ounces	4	■	■	30	38	■	■	64	72	■
Pounds	■	$\frac{1}{2}$	$1\frac{1}{2}$	■	■	3	$3\frac{3}{4}$	■	■	$5\frac{1}{4}$

6. Juanita was making biscuits for a party. She had to quadruple the recipe to make enough. The original recipe called for ten ounces of flour. How many pounds of flour should Juanita buy at the store?

7. It costs $15 to feed 3 guests at John's birthday party.

Guests	1	4	■	■	9	12	■	15	18	■
Cost	■	■	25	35	■	■	70	■	■	95

8. John's mother told him that she didn't want to spend more than $125 for John's birthday party. John has 24 students in his class. Will he be able to invite them all?

Write all of your answers on a separate sheet of paper.

Figure *ABCD* is a parallelogram. Find the measure of each angle.

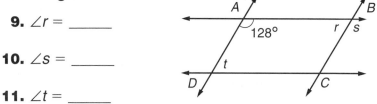

9. ∠*r* = _____

10. ∠*s* = _____

11. ∠*t* = _____

Draw a figure congruent to each given figure.

12.

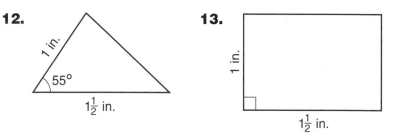

13.

Solve.

14. $\begin{array}{r} 1{,}018 \\ + 257 \end{array}$ **15.** $\begin{array}{r} 18 \\ * 75 \end{array}$ **16.** $\begin{array}{r} 113 \\ * 28 \end{array}$ **17.** $42\overline{)967}$

18. 18 + 29 + 36   **19.** 382 ÷ 7

20. 489 ÷ 21   **21.** 18 * 90

22. 16 + (3 * 75)   **23.** 109 − (312 − 286)

24. 239 ÷ 18   **25.** 780 ÷ 32

Practice Set 60

Write all of your answers on a separate sheet of paper.

Complete the table and find the missing rule. State the rule in words.

1. Rule: Brad jogs 4 miles per hour. **2.** Rule: _____

Time (hr) h	Distance (mi) 4 * h
2	8
3	12
▓	20
▓	40

Time (hr)	Earnings ($)
3	21
5	35
▓	59.5
▓	245

Solve.

3. $\frac{7}{8} + \frac{2}{8}$ **4.** $\frac{1}{3} - \frac{1}{3}$ **5.** $\frac{2}{4} + \frac{3}{4}$

6. $\frac{9}{8} - \frac{6}{8}$ **7.** $\frac{4}{5} + \frac{9}{5}$ **8.** $\frac{9}{7} - \frac{3}{7}$

9. $\frac{2}{6} + \frac{11}{6}$ **10.** $\frac{8}{1} - \frac{7}{1}$ **11.** $\frac{2}{2} + \frac{3}{2}$

12. $\frac{7}{9} - \frac{3}{9}$ **13.** $\frac{6}{9} + \frac{1}{9}$ **14.** $\frac{8}{9} - \frac{1}{9}$

Estimate each product.

15. 4.9 * 8.6 **16.** 4.32 * 8.16 **17.** 3.60 * 2.19

18. 3.2 * 1.6 **19.** 7.08 * 6.12 **20.** 9.28 * 3.10

21. 7.4 * 9.3 **22.** 1.2 * 3.81 **23.** 4.82 * 5.34

24. 16.1 * 1.4 **25.** 2.2 * 3.75 **26.** 2.16 * 4.81

27. 8.01 * 5.01 **28.** 6.8 * 1.25 **29.** 7.51 * 3.26

Use with or after Lesson 8.2.

Write all of your answers on a separate sheet of paper.

Solve using cross-products.

1. $\dfrac{3}{5} = \dfrac{x}{10}$ **2.** $\dfrac{1}{6} = \dfrac{b}{24}$ **3.** $\dfrac{3}{7} = \dfrac{18}{r}$

4. $\dfrac{2}{3} = \dfrac{n}{36}$ **5.** $\dfrac{6}{8} = \dfrac{54}{a}$ **6.** $\dfrac{4}{9} = \dfrac{12}{v}$

7. $\dfrac{6}{13} = \dfrac{c}{52}$ **8.** $\dfrac{4}{11} = \dfrac{n}{55}$ **9.** $\dfrac{1}{2} = \dfrac{a}{15}$

Write a proportion for each problem. Then use the proportion to solve the problem.

10. A 40-pound box of apples costs $24. What is the cost of 6 pounds of apples?

11. A case of 12 cans of soup costs $15.48. What is the cost of 2 cans of soup?

12. Mr. Evans drove 376 miles in 8 hours. What was his rate per hour?

13. A recipe for broccoli soup makes 5 servings and uses 3 cups of milk. How many servings of the soup could be made using 33 cups of milk?

Solve.

14. $-20 * 4$ **15.** $-32 \div 8$ **16.** $(-7) * (-9)$

17. $54 - (-6)$ **18.** $-15 + 2$ **19.** $-30 \div 5$

20. $49 \div (-7)$ **21.** $125 + (-20)$ **22.** $-56 - (-18)$

Write all of your answers on a separate sheet of paper.

Make name-collection boxes for the numbers below. Try to use parentheses and exponents in each name. Use as many different kinds of numbers and operations as you can. Make at least 7 different names for each number.

23. 42 **24.** 31 **25.** 27 **26.** 13

Solve each problem.

27. Andy works from 7:30 A.M. until 3:30 P.M. every day, 5 days a week. How many hours does Andy work each week?

28. Kelly went shopping and bought a pair of shoes for 20% off. The original price was $49.90. How much did Kelly pay for the shoes?

29. Melinda wanted to bake a cake. The recipe called for 1 pound of chocolate. If Melinda only had 3 ounces of chocolate, how much chocolate does she need to buy?

30. Laura walked a total of 14 blocks on Tuesday. She walked 4 blocks to the grocery store, 5 more blocks to the mall, and 3 blocks to the flower shop. How many blocks is it from the flower shop to Laura's home?

31. Max has $25.00 to spend on a bouquet of flowers. He wants the bouquet to have 4 roses. Roses cost $2.95 each. He also wants carnations in the bouquet. Carnations cost $1.25 each. How many carnations can he put in his bouquet?

Write all of your answers on a separate sheet of paper.

Write a proportion for each problem. Then use the proportion to solve the problem.

1. Ms. Lawrence has 36 music students. Two out of every three of her students study piano. How many students study piano?

2. Ruben earns 15 minutes of television time for each 30 minutes he spends on homework. If he spends 4 hours doing homework on the weekend, how much television time does he earn?

3. Complete the following table.

Decimal	Name in Words	Power of 10
0.02	two hundredths	$2 * 10^{-2}$
0.124	■	■
■	thirteen millionths	■
■	■	$1.08 * 10^{-4}$
■	seven thousand, two hundred sixty-eight ten thousandths	■
0.00007	■	■
■	■	$5.87 * 10^{-3}$
0.0042	■	■
■	two hundred forty-six thousandths	■
0.08003	■	■
■	■	$4 * 10^{-4}$

Write all of your answers on a separate sheet of paper.

Solve each problem.

1. If 6 puppies are $\frac{3}{4}$ of a litter, how many puppies are in the entire litter?

2. If 3 kittens are $\frac{3}{7}$ of a litter, how many kittens are in the entire litter?

3. If 2 eggs are $\frac{1}{2}$ of the eggs laid by a mother bird, how many eggs did the mother bird lay?

4. If you have read 36 pages or $\frac{1}{8}$ of the total pages in a book, how many pages are in the entire book?

5. If $3.88 is 12% of the cost of an answering machine, how much does the answering machine cost?

6. If 12 pounds of aluminum cans account for 40% of the weight of the materials recycled, how much do all the recycled materials weigh?

7. If 30 students are 15% of the students in the sixth-grade class, how many students are in the sixth-grade class?

8. If 82 miles are 27% of the miles the Davis family drove in one day, how many miles did they drive in one day?

Solve.

9. $6.3 * 10^{-5} = \blacksquare$

10. $\blacksquare = 95 * 6^3$

11. $25 * 10^5 = \blacksquare$

12. $1{,}757 * 10^{-4} = \blacksquare$

13. $3.4344 = 34{,}344 * 10^{\blacksquare}$

14. $\blacksquare = 80 * 10^{-6}$

15. $\blacksquare = 3.87 * 10^5$

16. $4.7 * 10^{\blacksquare} = 470{,}000{,}000$

Use with or after Lesson 8.7.

Write all of your answers on a separate sheet of paper.

Complete the table.

1. A copy machine was used to quadruple (4x) the size of geometric figures. Complete the table below.

Line Segment	Length of Original Figure	Length of Enlargement	Ratio of Enlargement to Original Figure
Radius	1 inch	■	■
Diameter	■	8 inches	■
Short side of parallelogram	■	7 inches	■
Long side of parallelogram	$3\frac{1}{4}$ inches	■	■
Diagonal of rectangle	$2\frac{5}{8}$ inches	■	■
Base of isosceles triangle	■	$1\frac{1}{2}$ inches	■
Height of isosceles triangle	$\frac{7}{8}$ inch	■	■
Side of regular octagon	■	10 inches	■

Solve.

2. $3x + 4 = 16$

3. $z - 17 = -3$

4. $21 - r = 19$

5. $4 - 3v = 16$

6. $9 + w = 201$

7. $\frac{n}{2} = 13$

8. $2y - 6 = 10$

9. $8c + 2c = 30$

10. $\frac{b}{4} = 7$

11. $4z + 4 = 16$

12. $8x - 2 = 22$

13. $5 + 4a = 13$

Write all of your answers on a separate sheet of paper.

Solve.

14. $\frac{4}{9} + \frac{8}{7}$ **15.** $\frac{1}{10} - \frac{4}{42}$ **16.** $\frac{13}{19} + \frac{5}{5}$

17. $\frac{7}{9} - \frac{2}{15}$ **18.** $\frac{6}{14} - \frac{1}{4}$ **19.** $\frac{2}{5} + \frac{6}{12}$

Find the perimeter of each figure.

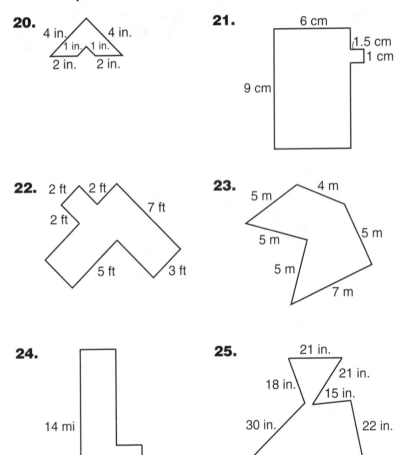

20. 4 in., 4 in., 1 in., 1 in., 2 in., 2 in.

21. 6 cm, 1.5 cm, 1 cm, 9 cm

22. 2 ft, 2 ft, 2 ft, 7 ft, 5 ft, 3 ft

23. 5 m, 4 m, 5 m, 5 m, 5 m, 7 m

24. 14 mi, 6 mi

25. 21 in., 21 in., 18 in., 15 in., 30 in., 22 in., 44 in.

Write all of your answers on a separate sheet of paper.

Determine the missing measurement for each set of similar figures.

1. $x = $ ■

2. $\angle t = $ ■

3. $y = $ ■

4. $r = $ ■

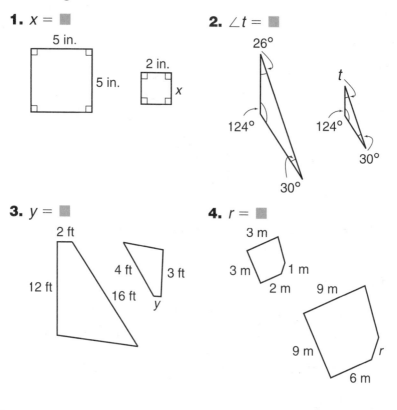

Decide whether each fraction is closest to 0%, 25%, 50%, 75%, or 100%.

5. $\frac{5}{61}$

6. $\frac{12}{13}$

7. $\frac{13}{28}$

8. $\frac{5}{19}$

9. $\frac{89}{96}$

10. $\frac{37}{75}$

11. $\frac{6}{23}$

12. $\frac{45}{58}$

13. $\frac{1}{56}$

14. $\frac{22}{81}$

15. $\frac{56}{73}$

16. $\frac{24}{49}$

Write all of your answers on a separate sheet of paper.

Each statement describes one of the spinners below. Write the letter of the spinner that each statement describes.

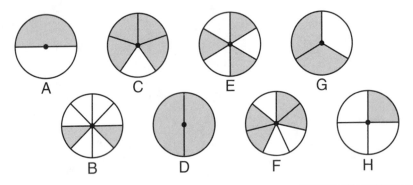

Example   The spinner will land on white $\frac{1}{5}$ of the time.
            Answer: Spinner C

---

17. The spinner will land on gray 4 out of 7 times.

18. The spinner will always land on gray.

19. The spinner will land on white 3 out of 6 times.

20. The spinner will land on gray 2 out of 8 times.

21. The spinner will land on gray 4 out of 5 times.

22. The spinner will land on gray 2 out of 3 times.

23. The spinner will land on gray 1 out of 4 times.

24. The spinner will never land on white.

25. The spinner will land on white 3 out of 4 times.

26. The spinner will land on white a little less than half of the time.

27. The spinner will land on gray 1 out of 2 times.

Use with or after Lesson 8.10.

Write all of your answers on a separate sheet of paper.

Complete. Give your answer in the hundredths.

1. $\frac{35}{15} = \frac{\blacksquare}{1}$

2. $\frac{57}{84} = \frac{\blacksquare}{1}$

3. $\frac{101}{59} = \frac{\blacksquare}{1}$

4. $\frac{74}{50} = \frac{\blacksquare}{1}$

5. $\frac{720}{990} = \frac{\blacksquare}{1}$

6. $\frac{250}{300} = \frac{\blacksquare}{1}$

7. $\frac{830}{670} = \frac{\blacksquare}{1}$

8. $\frac{456}{300} = \frac{\blacksquare}{1}$

Solve.

9. Robbie packed 4 t-shirts, 1 pair of shorts, and 1 pair of jeans. How many different outfits can he make from those clothes?

10. The Mountain Oak Middle School PTA is selling sweatshirts with the school logo. All the sweatshirt styles come in either blue or white. They can be ordered with or without hoods and with or without zippers. How many different sweatshirts can be ordered?

Complete the "What's My Rule?" tables.

11.

Rule	in	out
out = in / 30	180	
		24
	630	
		16
	4,500	

12.

Rule	in	out
	78	−11
	99	10
		14
	24	
	114	25

Write all of your answers on a separate sheet of paper.

Find the ratio of the length to the width for each rectangle.

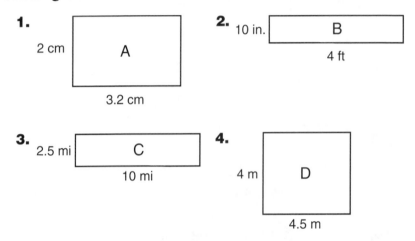

1.

2 cm | A |
3.2 cm

2. 10 in. | B |
4 ft

3. 2.5 mi | C |
10 mi

4. 4 m | D |
4.5 m

5. Which of the above rectangles most resembles a Golden Rectangle? Explain your answer.

A driver averages 60 miles per hour. Determine the number of hours needed to reach each destination.

6. Denver: 412 miles

7. Hollywood: 180 miles

8. Chicago: 68 miles

9. Philadelphia: 320 miles

10. Orlando: 804 miles

11. Phoenix: 72 miles

12. New York: 1,091 miles

13. Los Angeles: 625 miles

Divide.

14. $75.14 \div 3.4$

15. $13.23 \div 2.1$

16. $15.6 \div 0.3$

17. $357 \div 4.2$

18. $21.25 \div 1.7$

19. $156.4 \div 9.2$

Write all of your answers on a separate sheet of paper.

20. Write the letter for each ordered pair. You will read a
mystery message.

▦ ▦ ▦ ▦ ▦

(−5,7) (10,−2) (2,9) (6,−7) (−4,−5)

▦ ▦ ▦   ▦ ▦ ▦ ▦

(7,8) (9,6) (2,−2)   (5,9) (1,−1) (−8,2) (4,6)

▦ ▦ ▦ ▦ ▦ ▦ ▦ ▦ ▦

(7,5) (−8,2) (−6,−6) (8,−6) (6,−7) (5,−10) (−5,2) (−5,7) (10,2)

▦ ▦   ▦ ▦ ▦

(−8,−2) (8,0)   (2,−8) (1,1) (−7,5)

▦ ▦ ▦ ▦ ▦ ▦ ▦ ▦ ▦ ▦

(−1,−1) (7,−1) (−6,1) (6,−7) (−2,7) (−8,−2) (−5,2) (−6,−6) (2,−8) (−7,5)

▦ ▦ ▦ ▦ ▦

(6,2) (1,−4) (7,8) (−10,6) (9,10).

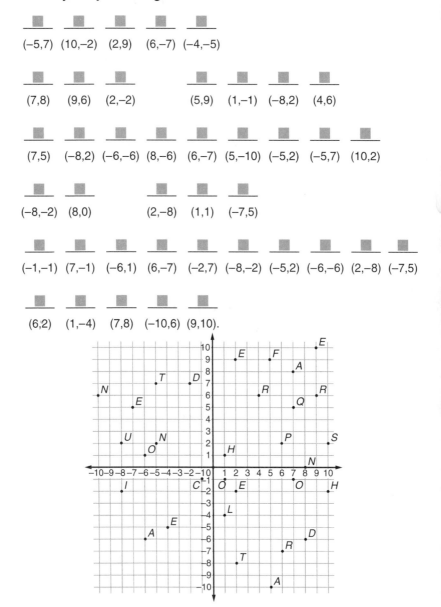

Write all of your answers on a separate sheet of paper.

Write the letter of the equivalent expression.

1. $(5 * 17) - (5 * 3)$ **A.** $(3 * 9) + (3 * r)$

2. $3 * (9 + r)$ **B.** $(17 + 3) * 5$

3. $(17 * 5) + (3 * 5)$ **C.** $(3 * 9) * r$

4. $3 * (9 * r)$ **D.** $5(17 - 3)$

5. $5 + (b + 16)$ **E.** $(b * 5) - (16 * 5)$

6. $(b - 16) * 5$ **F.** $(b + 5) + 16$

Divide. Show your work. Write your answers in simplest form.

Example $\frac{5}{9} \div \frac{2}{3}$

$$\frac{5}{9} \div \frac{2}{3} = \frac{5}{9} * \frac{3}{2} = \frac{15}{18}$$

Answer: $\frac{5}{6}$

7. $\frac{4}{7} \div \frac{6}{11}$ **8.** $2\frac{5}{8} \div \frac{1}{4}$

9. $3\frac{1}{7} \div 1\frac{2}{5}$ **10.** $3\frac{2}{7} \div 1\frac{6}{9}$

11. $6\frac{4}{8} \div 7\frac{1}{2}$ **12.** $4\frac{6}{7} \div 5\frac{3}{8}$

13. $1\frac{1}{10} \div 2\frac{3}{5}$ **14.** $6\frac{2}{3} \div 4\frac{1}{7}$

15. $3\frac{4}{9} \div 5\frac{1}{8}$ **16.** $4\frac{1}{2} \div 5$

17. $7\frac{2}{5} \div 9\frac{1}{10}$ **18.** $14\frac{2}{3} \div 8\frac{1}{6}$

19. $21\frac{2}{13} \div 1\frac{1}{26}$ **20.** $10\frac{4}{5} \div 9\frac{19}{20}$

Practice Set 69

Write all of your answers on a separate sheet of paper.

Simplify each expression by combining like terms.

1. $2x + 15 + 3x - 5$ **2.** $9t + 5t - 3t$

3. $-3y - 2y - y$ **4.** $3n - 2 + 2n + 5$

5. $(2\frac{1}{2})y - (\frac{1}{4})y$ **6.** $7x - 2x + 2 - x$

7. $12x + y - x + 6y$ **8.** $0.5n + 0.3n - 0.4n$

9. $9h + 4.5 - 7h + 1.75$ **10.** $3c + 6d - (-7c) + 8d$

Use a Venn Diagram to solve each problem.

11. Kevin's family participates in many sports. He has 8 people in his family. 5 play football, 6 play baseball, and 3 play both. How many of Kevin's family members only play one sport?

12. Jess works at a pool. 47 children are on the swim team. 12 children take diving lessons. 3 children take diving lessons and are on the swim team. How many children are only on the swim team?

13. Chau has a collection of 32 dolls. Each doll has black hair or brown eyes or both black hair and brown eyes. 18 of the dolls have black hair and 20 of the dolls have brown eyes. How many of Chau's dolls have both black hair and brown eyes?

Find the number.

14. 36 is 50% of what number?

15. What is 7% of 41?

16. 2 is 20% of what number?

17. 9 is 12% of what number?

Practice Set 69 (cont.)

Write all of your answers on a separate sheet of paper.

Copy and complete each table. Then find the per unit rates.

18. There are about 2.5 cm in 1 inch.

cm	2.5	5	■	■	8.75	■	■	■	■	■
in.	1	■	2.5	3	■	4	8	$\frac{1}{2}$	$\frac{3}{5}$	$\frac{4}{5}$

Per inch rate: ■ centimeters per inch
Per centimeter rate: ■ inches per centimeter

19. A cookie recipe calls for $\frac{3}{4}$ cup of sugar for 24 cookies.

Sugar (cups)	■	■	$1\frac{1}{2}$	■	■	$\frac{15}{16}$	■	$\frac{9}{16}$	■	1
Cookies	24	36	■	60	66	■	12	■	6	■

Per cookie rate: ■ cups of sugar per cookie
Per cup of sugar rate: ■ cookies per cup of sugar

Add or subtract.

20. $(-4) + (-6)$ **21.** $16 + (-14)$ **22.** $(-7) - (-51)$

23. $27 - (-4)$ **24.** $(-13) + (-9)$ **25.** $8 - (-14)$

26. $(-6) - 5$ **27.** $(-8) - (-3)$ **28.** $13 - (-4)$

29. $(-4) + (-17)$ **30.** $(-8) + 21$ **31.** $(-62) + 10$

32. $(-18) - (-14)$ **33.** $(-12) - 9$ **34.** $19 + (-6)$

35. $41 + (-21)$ **36.** $14 - (-7)$ **37.** $(-8) - (-15)$

38. $(-26) + 4$ **39.** $15 + (-2)$ **40.** $(-31) + 11$

41. $(-112) - 13$ **42.** $(-18) + 3$ **43.** $(-7) - 5$

   Use with or after Lesson 9.3.

Practice Set 70

SRB
112–115
234

Write all of your answers on a separate sheet of paper.

Simplify each expression by removing parentheses and combining.

1. $2(5 - a) + 5(1 + a)$ **2.** $r(3 + 7) - 5r$

3. $20(s - t) + 5s + 6t$ **4.** $3(m + 7) + 18m - 9$

5. $3(8 + t) + (-4t) + 12$ **6.** $4\frac{s}{7} - 2(\frac{s}{7} + 9)$

Use cross-multiplication to solve.

7. $\frac{4}{9} = \frac{12}{a}$ **8.** $\frac{18}{53} = \frac{r}{371}$ **9.** $\frac{5}{8} = \frac{s}{20}$

10. $\frac{57}{70} = \frac{t}{105}$ **11.** $\frac{18}{54} = \frac{b}{66}$ **12.** $\frac{9}{72} = \frac{13}{v}$

Solve.

13. $\frac{1}{2}$ of $\frac{1}{3}$ **14.** $\frac{1}{5}$ of $\frac{2}{7}$ **15.** $\frac{3}{10}$ of $\frac{2}{3}$

16. $\frac{1}{12}$ of $\frac{3}{8}$ **17.** $\frac{1}{7}$ of $\frac{1}{2}$ **18.** $\frac{2}{9}$ of $\frac{9}{25}$

Solve each problem.

19. There are 4 calories in each gram of protein. A piece of chicken has 20 grams of protein. How many protein calories are in the piece of chicken?

20. There are 4 calories in each gram of carbohydrate. If two cookies contain 40 grams of carbohydrate, how many carbohydrate calories do they contain?

21. There are 9 calories in each gram of fat. If there are 144 fat calories in the cookies, how many grams of fat do they contain?

Write all of your answers on a separate sheet of paper.

Write the letter of the equivalent equation.

1. $3b + 1 = 22$

2. $\frac{b}{12} + 3 = 1$

3. $7b - 6 = 29$

4. $6b + 10 = 46$

5. $\frac{b}{3} + 7 = 4$

A. $5b - 5 = 20$

B. $2b + 2 = -46$

C. $18 + b = 9$

D. $3(10) - 3(b) = 9$

E. $b * b = 36$

Describe in words the solution set for each inequality.

6. $t > 1$

7. $x < -1$

8. $3d \leq 21$

9. $\frac{d}{4} \geq 20$

Find the measure of each angle.

10. $\angle a =$ _____

11. $\angle b =$ _____

12. $\angle c =$ _____

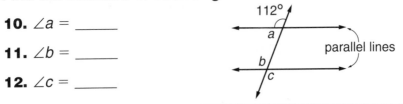

112°

a

b

c

parallel lines

Solve.

13. $17 * (-4)$

14. $(-11) * 5$

15. $(-15) * 4$

16. $(-6) * (-8)$

17. $(-19) * 8$

18. $(-16) * 3$

19. $(-21) * 12$

20. $3 * (-9)$

21. $(-17) * (-20)$

Write all of your answers on a separate sheet of paper.
Solve each equation. Combine like terms first.

Example

$$7t - 5 = 5t + 3$$
$$-5t \qquad -5t$$
$$2t - 5 = + 3$$
$$ + 5 \qquad + 5$$
$$2t = 8$$
$$\frac{2t}{2} = \frac{8}{2}$$
$$t = 4$$

1. $2 + n = 4$

2. $3 * m = 21$

3. $23 = a + 6$

4. $42 = 6 * k$

5. $4 - h = 8 - 2h$

6. $24 - b = b + 14$

7. $x + 3x = 16$

8. $d + 2^2 = 4d - 2$

9. $42 - 3 = 13y$

10. $f + 16 = 5f$

11. $37 + 13j = 27j - 5$

12. $3g - 18 = 6 - 5g$

13. $4s + 3 = 23 - s$

14. $14 - p = 2p - 4$

15. $r + 5 = 3r + 7$

16. $6 + 2q = 10 + q$

17. $8c * 3 = 48$

18. $4t * (3 + 2) = 16 + 4t$

19. $9t - c = 10t + 4c$

20. $6x + 4y = 8y + 3x$

21. $18x + 10 = 20x + 8$

22. $7w + 16y = 10w + 2y$

23. $14a + 6 = 34$

24. $21a - 16 = 0 - 11a$

Write all of your answers on a separate sheet of paper.

Make a tree diagram to solve each probability question.

25. 86 people went through this maze. How many people would you expect to end up in Room A?

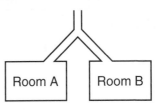

26. 72 people went through this maze. How many people would you expect to end up in Room A? Room B?

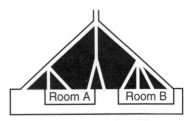

27. 24 people went through this maze. How many people would you expect to end up in Room A? Room B?

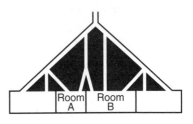

28. 54 people went through this maze. How many people would you expect to end up in Room A? Room B?

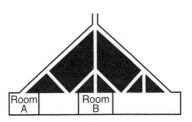

Write all of your answers on a separate sheet of paper.

Find the area of each figure below.

Area of a rectangle or square $= b * h$
Area of a circle $= \pi r^2$
Area of a triangle $= \frac{1}{2} b * h$
Area of a trapezoid $= (\frac{1}{2} b * h) + (l * w)$

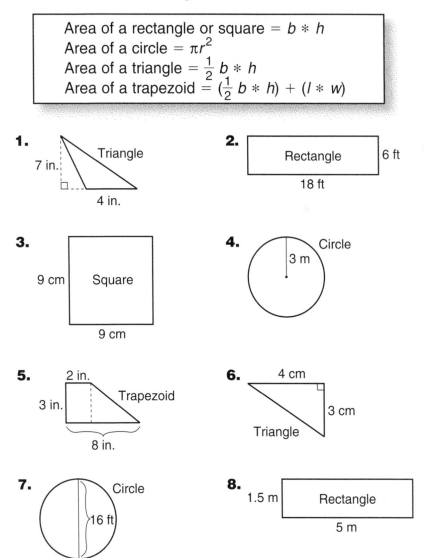

1. Triangle
7 in.
4 in.

2. Rectangle   6 ft
18 ft

3. 9 cm   Square
9 cm

4. Circle
3 m

5. 2 in.
3 in.   Trapezoid
8 in.

6. 4 cm
3 cm
Triangle

7. Circle
16 ft

8. 1.5 m   Rectangle
5 m

Write all of your answers on a separate sheet of paper.

Solve each problem.

9. Martha rode her bicycle 14 blocks to the library. It took her 10 minutes to ride to the library. How long did it take her to bicycle one block?

10. Sara lives 8 blocks from the library. She can walk 3 blocks in 12 minutes. Sara told Martha she would meet her at the library at 3:45. If she leaves her house at 3:15, will she be on time to meet Martha?

11. Jacob meets Martha and Sara at the library. He had rollerbladed to the library. He can rollerblade one block in one minute and 20 seconds. It took him 14 minutes and 40 seconds to get to the library. How many blocks does Jacob live from the library?

12. Manny used a skateboard to get to the library. It took him 6 minutes to skateboard 3 blocks. At that speed, how many blocks could Manny skateboard in one hour?

13. Dan's mother drove him to the library. He lives 3 miles away. On the way to the library, they stopped for 2 red lights that were each 45 seconds long. Dan's mom drove 30 miles per hour. How long did it take Dan to get to the library?

Divide.

14. $43.5 \div 2.9$

15. $9.28 \div 3.2$

16. $236.6 \div 9.1$

17. $16.17 \div 0.7$

18. $3.4 \div 6.8$

19. $134.4 \div 5.6$

Use with or after Lesson 9.8.

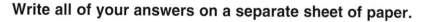

SRB
195 203
204 206

Write all of your answers on a separate sheet of paper.

Calculate the volume, perimeter, or circumference of each figure.

> Volume of a cylinder $= \pi r^2 h$
> Volume of a rectangular prism $= l * w * h$
> Volume of a sphere $= \frac{4}{3}\pi r^3$
> Circumference $= \pi * d$

1. Volume $= ?$

2 yd

4 yd   8 yd

2. Circumference $= ?$

4.5 in.

3. Volume $= ?$

$r = 7$ cm

4. Volume $= ?$

2 m

16 m

5. Perimeter $= ?$

14 in.

6 in.

7 in.

2 in.   2 in.   3 in.

4 in.

5 in.

5 in.

3 in.

6. Volume $= ?$

7 ft

5 ft   5 ft

7. Circumference $= ?$

10 cm

8. Volume $= ?$

6 m

3 m

Write all of your answers on a separate sheet of paper.

Evaluate each expression.

9. $(-31) + 43$ **10.** $(-14) - 46$ **11.** $(-6) * 9$

12. $17 + (-32)$ **13.** $3 * (-4)$ **14.** $12 \div (-3)$

15. $(-16) \div (-4)$ **16.** $(-12) - 54$ **17.** $(-24) \div 3$

18. $3 - (-4)$ **19.** $181 + (-68)$ **20.** $(-14) * (-8)$

21. $12 * (-6)$ **22.** $(-9) + (-18)$ **23.** $(-41) - (-3)$

24. $81 \div (-9)$ **25.** $(-24) * 8$ **26.** $17 - (-15)$

27. $(-76) \div (-19)$ **28.** $(-56) \div 8$ **29.** $(-39) + (-61)$

30. $(-64) \div 8$ **31.** $(-84) - (-76)$ **32.** $(-20) * 7$

Make name-collection boxes for the following numbers. Use as many different operations and numbers as possible. Make at least 7 different names for each number.

33. 21   **34.** 44   **35.** 77

36. 42.8   **37.** 25.9   **38.** 17.5

Multiply. Write each answer in simplest form.

39. $\frac{4}{9} * \frac{7}{6}$ **40.** $9\frac{3}{4} * 1\frac{1}{10}$ **41.** $\frac{3}{6} * \frac{4}{8}$

42. $6\frac{2}{5} * 2\frac{3}{6}$ **43.** $\frac{1}{4} * \frac{16}{17}$ **44.** $7\frac{1}{6} * 4\frac{1}{3}$

45. $\frac{8}{9} * \frac{3}{16}$ **46.** $3\frac{1}{4} * 1\frac{3}{7}$ **47.** $\frac{9}{10} * \frac{4}{11}$

48. $9\frac{6}{10} * 8\frac{1}{2}$ **49.** $\frac{2}{7} * \frac{1}{8}$ **50.** $4\frac{1}{6} * 3\frac{2}{4}$

51. $\frac{14}{15} * \frac{8}{7}$ **52.** $8\frac{1}{9} * 2\frac{1}{2}$ **53.** $\frac{6}{9} * \frac{3}{4}$

Write all of your answers on a separate sheet of paper.

Use the formula to evaluate each situation.

Formula: $3x + 9z$

1. $x = 4, z = 7$ **2.** $x = 9, z = 3$ **3.** $x = 5, z = 0$

Formula: $(c + 4) - b$

4. $c = 2, b = 3$ **5.** $c = -3, b = 11$ **6.** $c = 4, b = 6$

Formula: $t / 4 + s / 12$

7. $t = 8, s = 9$ **8.** $t = 3, s = -15$ **9.** $t = 0, s = 12$

Formula: $f * (g + 2)$

10. $f = 1, g = -1$ **11.** $f = 2, g = 3$ **12.** $f = 6, g = 0$

Determine whether each number sentence is true or false. If the number sentence is false, correct it to make the number sentence true.

13. $19 + (-7) * 2 = 5$

14. $76 = 8^2 + 3^2$

15. $3 * 12 + 4 = 8 - 6 * -8$

16. $16 \div 2 + 1 = 18 \div 3 + 3$

17. $4 + 9 = 19 - 6$

18. $3^2 + 4^2 = 7^2$

19. $81 \div 9 * 2 = 27 * \frac{2}{3}$

Write all of your answers on a separate sheet of paper.

Use the Pythagorean Theorem to determine the missing length of each triangle. Round your answer to the nearest tenth.

> Pythagorean Theorem
> $$a^2 + b^2 = c^2$$
> where a and b are the legs of the
> triangle and c is the hypotenuse

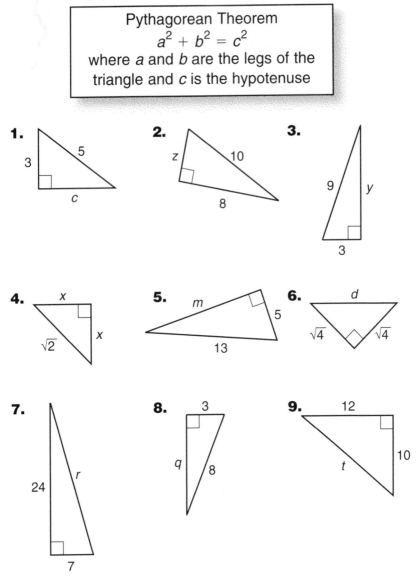

1. 3, 5, c

2. z, 10, 8

3. 9, y, 3

4. x, $\sqrt{2}$, x

5. m, 5, 13

6. d, $\sqrt{4}$, $\sqrt{4}$

7. 24, r, 7

8. 3, q, 8

9. 12, t, 10

Write all of your answers on a separate sheet of paper.

Complete each table.

10. Rule: $s = (19 - 4) + 2t$

t	s
−3	
0	
5	
$\frac{1}{2}$	
3	

11. Rule: $z = 4 * (c + 6)$

c	z
6	
9	
4	
0	
−1	

12. Rule: $(18 - p) * \frac{1}{2} = q$

p	q
	6
	1
	3
	0
	2

13. Rule: $7m * (2 + 3) = b$

m	b
	70
	0
	35
	105
	5

Tell if each statement about this spinner is *true* or *false*.

14. The spinner is more likely to land on white than on gray.

15. The probability of the spinner landing on white is 3 out of 5.

16. The probability of the spinner landing on gray is 6 out of 10.

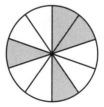

Write all of your answers on a separate sheet of paper.

Find the missing measurement for each similar figure.

1. $x = $ ■

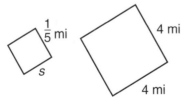

7 ft 8 ft 3 ft x

2. $t = $ ■

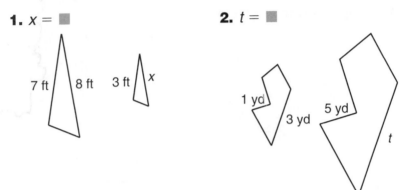

1 yd 3 yd 5 yd t

3. $d = $ ■

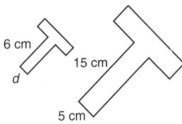

6 cm 15 cm 5 cm d

4. $r = $ ■

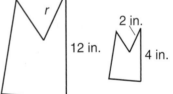

r 12 in. 2 in. 4 in.

5. $s = $ ■

$\frac{1}{5}$ mi 4 mi 4 mi s

6. $b = $ ■

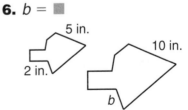

5 in. 2 in. 10 in. b

Write all of your answers on a separate sheet of paper.

Ellen made a table to show how she uses her allowance money each week.

7. How much is Ellen's allowance each week?

How I Use My Weekly Allowance	
Expense	**Amount**
Bus fare	$3.00
Lunches	$6.00
Savings	$1.00
Other	$2.00

8. What percent of her allowance does she use for
a. bus fare? **b.** lunches? **c.** savings? **d.** other?

9. Calculate the degree measures for each sector of a circle graph to show how Ellen uses her allowance.
a. bus fare **b.** lunches **c.** savings **d.** other

10. Draw a circle graph showing how Ellen uses her allowance.

Solve each equation.

11. $q + (7 * 3) = 31$

12. $7 * (n \div 8) = 14$

13. $8 = s \div 4 + 3$

14. $92 = r + 11$

15. $4w - 7 = w \div 2$

16. $20 \div w = w * 5$

17. $-12 = (104 \div 2) - t * 4$

18. $(3 * z) + 4 = 0.5 + (z * 5)$

Write all of your answers on a separate sheet of paper.

Tell whether each figure would tessellate. Write *yes* or *no*.

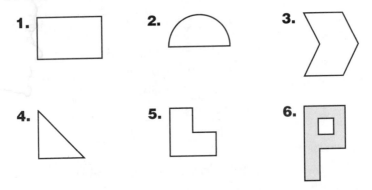

1.

2.

3.

4.

5.

6.

Complete the table. Then graph the data. Connect the points.

7. Peanuts cost $1.95 per pound.

   Rule: Cost = $1.95 per pound * the number of pounds

   Formula: $C = \$1.95 * w$

8. Plot a point to show the cost of 4.5 pounds of peanuts. How much do they cost?

Weight (lb)	Cost ($)
1	$1.95
0.5	
	$3.90
3	
8	

9. Cole, a large dog, can eat 3 cups of dog food per day.

   Rule: Amount of food = 3 cups per day * the number of days

   Formula: $F = d * 3$

10. Plot a point to show how many cups of food Cole ate in $3\frac{2}{3}$ days. How much did he eat?

Food (cups)	Days
9	
	$2\frac{1}{3}$
	$\frac{2}{3}$
10	
	4

Use with or after Lesson 10.2.

Write all of your answers on a separate sheet of paper.

Give the coordinates of the ordered pair associated with each letter.

11. *H*　　　　**12.** *K*　　　　**13.** *C*　　　　**14.** *A*

15. *D*　　　　**16.** *S*　　　　**17.** *T*　　　　**18.** *G*

19. *Y*　　　　**20.** *V*　　　　**21.** *L*　　　　**22.** *I*

23. *J*　　　　**24.** *B*　　　　**25.** *W*　　　　**26.** *X*

27. *Q*　　　　**28.** *R*　　　　**29.** *M*　　　　**30.** *P*

31. *Z*　　　　**32.** *E*　　　　**33.** *F*　　　　**34.** *N*

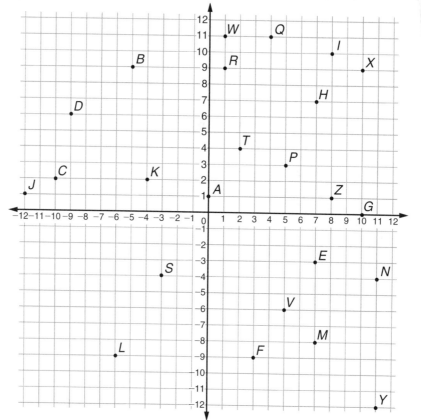

Write all of your answers on a separate sheet of paper.

Tell whether each dotted line is a line of symmetry.
Write *yes* or *no*.

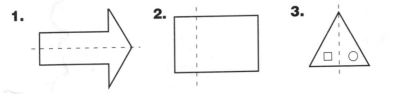

1.

2.

3.

Write and solve an equation for each situation.

4. Cassie had $20. She bought 3 copies of a book for
b dollars each. She had $2 left. How much did each
book cost?

5. On Saturday Brad mowed 3 lawns for *d* dollars each.
He spent $5 for lunch. At the end of the day he had
$40. Much did he earn mowing each lawn?

Choose the formula that describes the rule. Write the
letter of your choice.

6. **a.** $2m - 3.192 = n$
b. $m + 1.28 = n$
c. $m * 1.4 = n$

in (*m*)	out (*n*)
3.2	4.48
5.32	7.448
7.6	10.64
10.1	14.14
2	2.8

7. **a.** $v * v = k$
b. $v^3 = k$
c. $5v + 100 = k$

v	*k*
2	8
3	27
5	125
7	343
8	512

Use with or after Lesson 10.3.

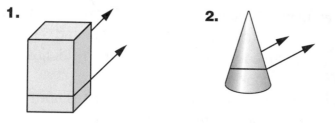
Write all of your answers on a separate sheet of paper.

Describe the shape of each cross-section.

1.

2.

Estimate equivalent percents for each fraction.

3. $\frac{8}{9}$ **4.** $\frac{29}{99}$ **5.** $\frac{6}{33}$ **6.** $\frac{70}{201}$

7. $\frac{2}{23}$ **8.** $\frac{19}{48}$ **9.** $\frac{12}{37}$ **10.** $\frac{7}{11}$

Copy and complete each table. Then find the per unit rates.

11. A tree grows $\frac{1}{2}$ inch in diameter per year.

Inches	$\frac{1}{2}$	■	$3\frac{1}{2}$	■	■	■	4	■	$\frac{3}{4}$	$\frac{1}{4}$
Year	■	2	■	4	5	9	■	7	■	■

Per year rate: ■ inches of growth per year
Per inch rate: ■ years per inch of growth

12. A printer can produce 50 pages in 2 minutes.

Pages	■	150	175	■	75	■	200	25	■
Minutes	2	■	■	5	■	1	■	■	7

Per minute rate: ■ pages printed per minute
Per page rate: ■ minutes per page

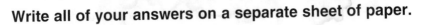
Write all of your answers on a separate sheet of paper.

Use a Venn Diagram to solve each problem.

13. Graham was having a tea party. 14 friends came over to his house. 8 friends wanted only tea, and 5 friends wanted both tea and cookies. How many friends wanted just cookies?

14. Brenda needed volunteers to wash dishes and set tables before the fundraiser dinner. 61 people volunteered. 38 people volunteered to just set the table. 17 people volunteered to wash dishes and set the table. How many people volunteered to just wash dishes?

15. The sixth-grade class at Taylorville has 45 students. 22 students are in the band, and the rest are in the math club. 10 students are in the band only. How many students are in both the math club and band?

Use the distributive property to rewrite each expression. Then simplify.

> **Example** $7 * (3 + 4) =$
> $(7 * 3) + (7 * 4) =$
> $21 + 28 = 49$

16. $(4 + 2) * 9$

17. $(4 + 1) * 2$

18. $25 * (7 + 10)$

19. $21 * (3 - 1)$

20. $14 * (8 + 5)$

21. $(84 - 6) * \frac{1}{2}$

22. $(91 - 7) * 2$

23. $(8 + 17) * 4$

24. $7 * (30 + 6)$

25. $(17 - 16) * 8$

26. $(7 + 3) * m$

27. $v * (2 + 1)$

28. $d * (f - a)$

29. $b * (a + c)$

Use with or after Lesson 10.4.